DANCING AT LUGHNASA

D1214967

Ireland Into Film

Series editors:
Keith Hopper (text) and Gráinne Humphreys (images)

Ireland Into Film is the first project in a number of planned
collaborations between Cork University Press and the Film
Institute of Ireland. The general aim of this publishing initiative
is to increase the critical understanding of 'Irish' Film (i.e. films
made in, or about, Ireland). This particular series brings together
writers and scholars from the fields of Film and Literary Studies
to examine notable adaptations of Irish literary texts.

Other titles available in this series:

The Dead (Kevin Barry)
December Bride (Lance Pettitt)
This Other Eden (Fidelma Farley)
The Informer (Patrick F. Sheeran)
The Quiet Man (Luke Gibbons)
The Field (Cheryl Temple Herr)

Forthcoming titles:

Nora (Gerardine Meaney)
The Butcher Boy (Colin MacCabe)

Ireland Into Film

DANCING AT LUGHNASA

Joan FitzPatrick Dean

CORK UNIVERSITY PRESS

in association with
THE FILM INSTITUTE OF IRELAND

First published in 2003 by
Cork University Press
Cork
Ireland

© Joan FitzPatrick Dean 2003

All rights reserved. No part of this book may be reprinted or reproduced or utilized
by any electronic, mechanical or other means, now known or hereafter invented,
including photocopying or recording or otherwise, without either the prior written
permission of the Publishers or a licence permitting restricted copying in Ireland
issued by the Irish Copyright Licensing Agency Ltd, The Irish Writers' Centre, 19
Parnell Square, Dublin 1.

The author has asserted her moral rights in this work.

British Library Cataloguing in Publication Data
A CIP catalogue record for this book is available from the British Library.

ISBN 1 85918 361 1

Typesetting by Red Barn Publishing, Skeagh, Skibbereen

Reprinted in 2005 by Lightning Souce, UK

Ireland Into Film receives financial assistance from
the Arts Council/An Chomhairle Ealaíon and the Film Institute of Ireland

*For my sister Margaret
and my brother Christopher*

CONTENTS

LIST OF ILLUSTRATIONS

Acknowledgements

I am grateful to Helen Hewson and Noel Kissane at the National Library of Ireland for providing access to the materials in the Brian Friel Papers. I am happy to acknowledge the support of a Faculty Research Grant from the School of Graduate Studies at the University of Missouri, Kansas City.

I enjoyed the helpful advice of my colleagues Linda Voigts, Lois Spatz and Jeff Rydberg-Cox. Bríd Brennan, Frank McGuinness and Naoise Barry generously discussed their experience with me. Tom Poe, Marianne Wells and Karen Vandevelde read sections of the manuscript and offered valuable suggestions. My editors, Keith Hopper and Gráinne Humphreys, were extremely helpful and always encouraging. In helping me with the typing, proofreading and editing, my daughter Flannery made work a joy. I am especially grateful to Lance Pettitt and Jack Cashill, who read the entire manuscript, although any errors are mine alone.

The editors would also like to thank Noel Pearson and Annmarie Naughton (Ferndale Films), Marie Rooney (Gate Theatre), Tom Lawlor, Metro-Goldwyn Mayer Inc, Woody Allen, Kenneth Trodd, Gráinne MacLochlainn, the National Library of Ireland, Sheila Pratschke, Lar Joyce, Michael Davitt, Luke Dodd, Dennis Kennedy, Kevin Rockett, Ellen Hazelkorn, Seán Ryder, Brian Jackson and St. Cross College (Oxford).

Special thanks to Ben Cloney, Stephen Moynihan, Antoinette Prout and the staff of the Irish Film Archive.

All images may be sourced at the Irish Film Centre Archive.

INTRODUCTION

We are world citizens as well as Irishmen.
Mervyn Wall, September 1936[1]

Dancing at Lughnasa exists in several versions: Brian Friel's play (as a typescript draft, as a published play and as multiple unique performances); Frank McGuinness's screenplay; and Pat O'Connor's film. Although the screenplay is faithful to the play and the film's final cut is very close to the published screenplay, crucial differences exist among these versions. In its broadest outline, as the story of unmarried women who eke out a modest but not unhappy existence, *Dancing at Lughnasa* enjoyed enormous success on stage in and beyond Ireland. First produced in 1990, Friel's highly theatrical play is best remembered for the sisters's frenzied dance, a brief Dionysian release from life's demands and disappointments. Together with their brother,

Plate 1.   Kate returning home by bike

a priest returned from the African missions, and the non-marital child they raise, the five sisters challenge preconceptions of Irish life in 1936.

As remote as the worlds of theatre and film production often are, Noel Pearson, the Abbey's chairman in 1990 and eight years later the film's producer, provides a link between the stage play and film. Pearson envisioned a cinematic adaptation of Friel's play from very early on and anticipated the film's wide appeal to diasporic audiences: 'nearly everyone [in Ireland] has a sister or aunt who lived like that. The provincialism of the story also makes it universal so I think it will appeal further afield than Ireland'.[2] Despite the success of *Dancing at Lughnasa* on stage, on film that appeal faltered.

The film's production followed a model set by that of *My Left Foot* (1989), directed by Jim Sheridan and also produced by Pearson, which, with its eight nominations and two Academy Awards, tapped a lucrative transatlantic market for Irish film. *My Left Foot* offered superficial comparisons with *Dancing at Lughnasa*: Christy (Daniel Day-Lewis) was born only three years after the narrator in *Dancing at Lughnasa*; both films dwell on the formative experiences of childhood and underscore the community's intolerance; and both were adapted from successful autobiographical or semi-autobiographical works. Like *My Left Foot*, *Dancing at Lughnasa* recruited an international cast; only one member of the Irish ensemble that created Friel's play on stage, Bríd Brennan, was cast in the film. Meryl Streep brought her prestige and box office potential. The play's diegetic music yielded to a lush, heavily orchestrated score by Bill Whelan, whose music for *Riverdance* had reached vast, international audiences. All of these changes aimed at increasing the film's appeal and box office.

In the process, the uniquely theatrical elements of Friel's play succumbed to the Classical Hollywood Style.[3] Whereas Friel deployed a variety of theatrical strategies to subvert realism, O'Connor's film subordinated them to invisible editing and seamless, logical sequences. The cinematic space, especially the landscape, in O'Connor's film was so stable as to seem inert. And the film euphemized the women's suffering to provide a much happier ending. Despite an aggressive and canny marketing campaign, these tactics failed. Made at a cost of over $12 million, in its theatrical release *Dancing at Lughnasa* did not come close to returning its production budget.[4]

The central tensions in *Dancing at Lughnasa* are between the Mundys and their society, between Catholicism and 'pagan' beliefs. The pagan, both the African beliefs (mementos of which Father Jack carries back to Ballybeg) and the remnants of Celtic mythology that survive in the Lughnasa celebrations, appears only in occluded or vestigial form. Friel himself describes the pagan as a requisite for humanity: 'I think there's a need for the pagan in life . . . If too much obeisance is offered to manners, then in some way we lose or suppress the grumbling and dangerous beast that's underneath the ground. This denial is what causes the conflict.'[5] Both film and play convey these tensions between the family and their community, yet the film is less successful in incorporating the pagan as a human prerequisite. The contrast between the theatrical and cinematic modes of presentation is nowhere more evident than in the very different treatments of the narrator and the sisters's dance.

Vivian Sobchack notes that contemporary film treatments of history, such as *Forrest Gump* (1994) and *Ragtime* (1997), partake of a 'contemporary history [that] is practiced and written not in the certitude of corresponding "historical facts" but rather in the productive unreliability and partiality of lived and invented memories, murmurs, nostalgias, stories, myths, and dreams'.[6] A self-conscious, perhaps postmodern, construction of the past, the stage play draws on Friel's own life and Irish history selectively and unexpectedly, often to link the present with the past. However, such unreliability and uncertainty on stage yield to stability and certitude in the film. These versions of *Dancing at Lughnasa* map the differences between theatre-going and film-going and between what was embraced as distinctly Irish at the beginning and end of the 1990s.

1

AN ANACHRONISTIC PAST

Dancing at Lughnasa is the most autobiographical of Brian Friel's plays. Like his narrator, Michael, Friel was seven years old in 1936, the year Father Jack returned to his sisters in Ballybeg. Friel dedicated his play to his mother's sisters, 'In memory of those five brave Glenties women', whose names remain unchanged. As a boy, Friel spent summer vacations with them at their home, The Laurels. He traces the genesis of *Dancing at Lughnasa* to a conversation with his Field Day co-director and friend, Tom Kilroy:

> I was at a play at the National Theatre with the playwright Thomas Kilroy. We walked across the Waterloo Bridge and up the Strand. It was about eleven-thirty at night, and there were homeless sleeping in the doorways. Tom said, 'If you talked to those people, I'm sure many of them are Irish.' And I said, 'I had two aunts, who, I think, ended up something like that.' He said, 'Why don't you write about that?' So that's how it began: backward.[7]

Kilroy recalls that, like Michael, Friel 'told the story of himself as a young man setting off for London to search for the two aunts who had left Donegal years before. What he found was destitution.'[8]

Friel's mother's family included other sisters and brothers, one of whom serves as the inspiration for Father Jack. Described in his obituary in the *Derry Journal* as 'The Wee Donegal Priest', Father Bernard MacLoone worked in Nyenga, Uganda, between 1911 and 1946.[9] Despite the strong similarities between Friel's uncle and Father Jack – both spent most of their adult lives as 'leper priests' in Africa, suffered from malaria and ended their lives with their sisters in Donegal – they are not to be confused. That Friel retained his aunts' names but changed Jack's indicates the distance between Friel's uncle and his character. What is more, Friel's uncle did not return to Ireland until 1946 and died thirteen years after Father Jack.

Just as it is mistaken to identify Father Jack as Friel's uncle, it is misleading to identify Michael as Friel. Friel was not a non-marital

Plate 2.   Brian Friel

child; his mother did not work in a factory. His father – a committed nationalist, teacher and school principal – was a very unlikely model for the Welsh gramophone salesman. There were, in addition, two incomes in the household of his Glenties aunts; not one but two of his aunts taught in school. Although Friel identifies 'Mundy [as] the American name for MacCloone [sic]'[10] (his mother's maiden name), there are obvious and telling departures from fact. Friel's treatment of the past, here as elsewhere, is mediated by personal memory and artistic imperatives:

> What is a fact in the context of autobiography? A fact is something that happened to me or something I experienced. It can also be something I thought happened to me, something I thought I experienced. Or indeed an autobiographical fact can be pure fiction and no less true or reliable for that.[11]

In *Philadelphia, Here I Come!* (1963) the May afternoon Gar spent fishing with his father in a blue boat fifteen years earlier, itself based on Friel's analogous memory,[12] dates from a time when he was the same age as Michael. Friel once told an interviewer: 'They say, you know, that nothing important ever happens to you after you're ten or so. That could be very true. I'm a very strong believer in this theory.'[13] Friel's account of his experience as a teacher corroborates how strongly Friel privileges childhood experience. Dismissive of the seven years spent teaching intermediate students for the Christian Brothers, he describes his three years of primary teaching as an 'epiphany'.[14] Friel evocatively, although rarely nostalgically, uses the time of his boyhood in other plays: in *Wonderful Tennessee* (1993), for example, drunken pilgrims returning from the Eucharistic Congress in 1932 murder Sean O'Boyle.

Friel's relationship to his source materials – literary, musical, folkloric, historical and autobiographical – is one in which he vigorously asserts his freedom as an artist. Employing sources ranging from anthropology and folklore to history and science writing, Friel eclectically draws on published materials. George Steiner's *After Babel*, P. J. Dowling's *The Hedge Schools of Ireland* and John Andrews' *A Paper Landscape* inform *Translations*, the last of these sources selectively and controversially.[15] *Making History* (1988) relies on Seán O'Faoláin's *The Great O'Neill* (1942) and Kilroy's *The O'Neill* (1969). Oliver Sacks's 'To See and Not See' is credited as an inspiration for *Molly Sweeney* (1995). Friel's relationship to his principal sources in *Dancing at Lughnasa* – Máire MacNeill's *The Festival of Lughnasa* and his memory of his aunts contextualized in his retrospective reading of Ireland in the 1930s – also submit to his insistence on the 'imperatives of fiction'.[16] Although Donegal residents who knew his aunts have no recollection of Lughnasa ('I never heard of the festival of Lughnasa in me life,' says Dr Malachy McCloskey, at 77 [in 1992] one the [Glenties'] older residents. 'And we wouldn't be dancing round fires or anything like that'[17]), Friel has always argued that his artistic purposes take precedence over rude fact.

With the exception of his second play, *The Enemy Within* (1962), Friel employed present-day or near contemporaneous settings in his plays of the 1960s and 1970s. In setting *Translations* (1980) in pre-famine Donegal, Friel began an interrogation of Irish history. *Making History* (1988) is set in the late sixteenth and early seventeenth centuries, *Dancing at Lughnasa* in 1936; his adaptation of Charles Macklin's *London Vertigo* (1991) is set in the time of its original composition: 1761. Friel's engagement with the processes of historiography is most evident in *Making History* when Archbishop Lombard ponders the accuracy of his account of Hugh O'Neill and echoes Friel's view of autobiographical fact: 'Are truth and falsity the proper criteria? I don't know. Maybe when the time comes my first responsibility will be to tell the best possible narrative. Isn't that what history is, a kind of story-telling? . . . maybe imagination will be as important as information'. Friel's treatment of the past is often anachronistic, employing language ('venue', 'Pragmatism', 'guerrilla warfare' in *Making History*),[18] technologies and attitudes that disclose his dramatic situations as contemporary constructions of the past. *Dancing at Lughnasa* partakes of comparable creative anachronisms to suggest strong affinities between the lives of his characters and those of his audience, between Ireland in 1936 and in 1990.

Friel's shift away from contemporaneous dramatic settings occured at the same time that he co-founded the Field Day Theatre Company in 1980. Field Day's enterprises quickly expanded beyond premièring and touring plays to publishing pamphlets and, under the editorship of Seamus Deane, *The Field Day Anthology of Irish Writing*. Seeking to foster an understanding of contemporary dilemmas through an understanding and a reimagining of cultural traditions, Field Day hoped to 'enrich and illuminate awareness of the complex nature of the Irish tradition in writing'.[19] The past – its cultural and political legacies – would illumine the present. By the late sixties, Irish playwrights were engaged in an analogous recovery of Irish history. Since Tom Murphy's *Famine* (1970), Irish dramatists have reclaimed and reimagined historical situations with increasing frequency, typically with the objective of explicating their contemporary dilemma. Friel's friend and colleague Tom Kilroy had worked in this vein in *The O'Neill, Talbot's Box* (1979; set in the 1920s), *Double Cross* (1986; set in the 1940s) and *The Madam Macadam Travelling Theatre* (1992; also set in the 1940s). Stewart Parker's three history plays, *Northern Star* (1984; set with 'deliberate anachronisms and historical shifts' around 1798), *Heavenly Bodies* (1986; set in 1890) and *Pentecost* (1987; set in 1974), were 'conceived and written, in consecutive order, between 1983 and 1987, as a common enterprise';[20] Frank McGuinness's *Observe the Sons of Ulster Marching Towards the Somme* (1985; set in 1916) and Sebastian Barry's *The Prayers of Sherkin* (1990; set in 1890) and subsequent dramatic explorations of his imagined ancestors all see the past as prologue. Benedetto Croce's analysis of historiography is equally applicable to these playwrights: 'The practical requirements which underlie every historical judgment give to all history the character of "contemporary history", because, however remote in time events thus recounted may seem to be, the history in reality refers to present needs and present situations wherein those events vibrate'.[21] Discovering historical events that resonate within the present, these Irish history plays engender a perspective that reflects the time of their composition as well as the past and thus, for some, convey a sense of the continuous past.

Dancing at Lughnasa is (like Kilroy's *Double Cross*) rare among these Irish history plays by mapping not a uniquely Irish context, but an international one. For film audiences, there are few visual clues in *Dancing at Lughnasa* beyond a title identifying 'Donegal – 1936' to designate this time. Indeed, the film's *mise-en-scène* might evoke any time after the initiation of radio broadcasting in 1926 and before the 1960s. Unlike the film, Friel treats 1936 as a subject that not only speaks directly to his audiences in the late 1980s and early 1990s, but advances the task of re-reading the past: 'I think one should look back on the process of history with some kind of coolness. The only merit in looking back is to understand, how you are and where you are at this moment'.[22]

Friel's choice of 1936 situates the action of *Dancing at Lughnasa* in a specific historical moment in his lifetime, as well as in Ireland's and the world's history. For the family, as for much of Europe, it is a time of upheaval and transition. The long-anticipated reunion of the sisters with their older brother will last less than a year: Jack will die; Rose and Agnes will emigrate; Kate will lose her job as a teacher. Writing *Translations* a decade earlier, Friel indicated his attraction to a similar time: 'In Ballybeg, at the point when the play [*Translations*] begins, the cultural climate is a dying climate – no longer quickened by its past, about to be plunged almost overnight into an alien future. The victims in this situation are the transitional generation.'[23] Similarly, Friel's preface to Charles McGlinchey's *The Last of the Name* is especially apposite to *Dancing at Lughnasa* and worth quoting at length:

McGlinchey's memoir is a chronicle of a period of profound transition in this island and he himself is a Janus figure facing in two directions. The historian or sociologist can arbitrarily choose almost any period in the history of a society and demonstrate that at that particular time significant changes took place in the life of a people. If the chosen period were McGlinchey's life (1861–1954) attention would rightly focus on issues like Home Rule and the land wars, the rise and fall of Parnell, the Rising of 1916, two world wars, the atomic bomb. McGlinchey does not mention even one of these events. They are overlooked in a manner that is almost Olympian. They do not merit his notice. But by his concentration on the everyday, the domestic, the familiar, the nuance of a phrase, the tiny adjustment to a local ritual, the momentous daily trivia of the world of his parish, he does give us an exact and lucid picture of profound transition: a rural community in the process of shedding the last vestiges of the Gaelic past and of an old Christianity that still cohabited with an older paganism, and of the community coming to uneasy accommodation with the world of today.[24]

Conspicuous by their absence are references to Irish affairs in 1936. In the 1930s de Valera undertook what Alvin Jackson calls 'the meticulous demolition of the constitution of 1922'.[25] Indeed, by 1937 de Valera had systematically purged what he found most offensive in the Irish Free State: the Oath of Allegiance, the Seanad (or Senate) and the office of Governor General. Neither play nor film mentions the outlawing of the IRA (again) in 1936, the abolition of the Seanad in May of that year, the Free State's criminalization of the importation or sale of any form of birth control the previous year, or the passage of the Legitimacy Act (1930), which 'legitimated' children whose parents subsequently married. Although Gerry plans to travel to fight in the Spanish Civil War, we hear nothing of Eoin O'Duffy's more (in)famous Irish Brigade, which fought for Franco against the International Brigade. Absent is the fact that 'by the end of the summer of 1936 the Irish Christian Front's huge pro-Franco rallies were sweeping Ireland'.[26] Nor is there mention of de Valera's call for sanctions against Italy after it invaded Abyssinia. With the exception of the song lyric concerning de Valera, *Dancing at Lughnasa* makes scant reference to events in contemporaneous Ireland. Perhaps most noteworthy is the omission of any reference to the Irish Constitution which the Dáil and a public referendum would ratify by a slim majority within a year.

These lacunae suggest a perspective of what Richard Kearney describes as a 'postnationalist Ireland', a view that resonated with Irish audiences in the early 1990s.[27] The situation of Danny Bradley, whose wife left him and their three children, would have been seen by the play's first Irish audiences in light of the defeated 1986 referendum that failed to overturn the constitutional ban on divorce. (The ban was overturned by a very narrow margin in 1995.) Similarly, 13.8% of Irish children under 16, like Michael and the Bradley children, lived in single-parent households in 1996. In the 1990s, as throughout Europe and the world, the rate of non-marital births in Ireland soared. By 1998, the rate in Ireland (28.3%) exceeded the European average (22%) and has since continued its steep rise. In its treatment of divorce, non-marital births and family formation, the vision of *Dancing at Lughnasa* is bifocal, looking back to 1936 as well as at 1990. As elsewhere, Friel effectively deploys creative anachronism to remind his audience of its link with the past.

Many recent accounts describe Ireland in the 1930s as the worst of the twentieth century's bad old days. In 1936, de Valera's Fianna Fáil government (1932–48) was closing itself off – economically through a trade war and culturally through an ever-narrowing self-definition. Terence Brown sees an atmosphere marked by an 'almost Stalinist antagonism to modernism, to surrealism, free verse, symbolism, and the modern cinema . . . combined with prudery . . . and a deep reverence for the past'.[28] Paul Scott Stanfield writes that in the 1930s 'the Irish writer was so hampered by the official censorship of the state and the unofficial censorship of various religious and political watchdog associations that it was impossible for him to live by distinctive Irish literature . . . Irish spirituality seemed confined to Jansenistical piety and commercialised pilgrimages.'[29] Caitriona Clear observes, 'there was strong and overt hostility to women throughout the period'.[30] The period after Irish independence is often characterized by an intensification of the repression of women and an acceleration of ecclesiastical intervention in the state. Bronwen Walter, for instance, asserts that 'the establishment of Irish independence increased the limitations on women's lives . . . In 1923, very soon after the establishment of the Free State, a "marriage bar" was introduced prohibiting married women from remaining in paid employment after marriage in certain occupations'.[31] Brian Fallon, however, amends the image of Ireland in the 1930s 'as dominated by insularity, defense-minded nationalism, the Church, censorship, a retreat from the outer world. [An] attitude has fossilised into a kind of dogma . . . '[32] Fallon describes a very different cultural landscape: the heyday of the Gate Theatre, the founding of *The Bell* and the short-lived *Ireland To-Day*. Joost Augusteijn similarly argues that 'the Free State was not just the insular self-obsessed and culturally barren society it has often been portrayed as'.[33] Clear notes that Ireland was hardly alone in its social policies:

> The idea that de Valera and the Catholic hierarchy – in particular the Catholic Archbishop John Charles McQuaid – were, as a result of their study of Catholic teaching, largely responsible for the notion that a woman's place was exclusively in the home, and that they embedded this idea into the Irish Constitution of 1937, is not the whole truth . . . Throughout the 1930s, policies, forged by strong political ideologies, were

> put in place in a wide range of countries to encourage women
> to stay in the home and to rear children.[34]

J. H. Whyte, moreover, asserts that, on two points, a secular definition of marriage and the recognition of other religions, the 1937 Constitution 'did not measure up to what Catholic authorities might have desired . . . neither Cardinal MacRory, then the Archbishop of Armagh, nor Pope Pius XI were altogether satisfied with the text'.[35] With specific reference to the film *Dancing at Lughnasa*, Maeve Binchy offers the more subjective view of Ireland in the 1930s as 'a world in which a woman was ashamed to accept a promotion or a good job because it could be considered antisocial – the man who might have gotten that job and supported a family with the wage would now be forced to emigrate'.[36]

At first glance, the Mundys appear to incarnate de Valera's ideal of frugal self-sufficiency in rural, Catholic Ireland, but the family is surprisingly, even anachronistically, unconventional for its time and place. Kate earns a living outside the home in one of the few careers open to Irish women in the 1930s; another sister cares nothing for the religious or social strictures against her affection for a married man; they are not above rude language such as 'Bastard' (BF, p. 6 and p. 34) and 'bitch' (BF, p. 34/McG, p. 46).[37] Moreover, all of the sisters are sexual beings. If forced to choose, Maggie would gladly take a fat 52-year-old widower over her much-loved Wild Woodbines. Chris enjoys a long-term sexual relationship with Gerry and yet is not compelled to accept his offer of marriage. Rose's fling with Danny Bradley is perhaps the most perilous of all the relations with men. Jack hopes that all his sisters will have children, in or out of wedlock. In Friel's play, Maggie tells Jack: 'We're hoping that you'll hunt about and get men for all of us' (BF, p. 40). He might not, but he could find one husband whom they all could share: 'I couldn't promise four men but I should be able to get one husband for all of you . . . That's our system and it works very well. One of you would be his principal wife and live with him in his largest hut . . . And the other three of you he'd keep in his enclosure' (BF, p. 63). Not only Chris and Rose, but four of the women are linked with a potential lover: Maggie with Brian McGuinness, who emigrated to Australia years ago, and Kate with Curly McDaid and Austin Morgan. The males, Michael and Father Jack, are both a liability and a great blessing to the family: the illegitimate Michael leaves the family vulnerable to gossip; that Father Jack had 'gone native' provokes the local parish priest to dismiss the blameless Kate from her teaching position. Males are dangerous to the Mundy sisters because they reveal the women's sexuality.

Embodying authoritarian if not patriarchal judgement, Kate knows that any expression of the women's sexuality is fraught with danger. Although in 1936 most rural Irish women were unmarried at the age of thirty, the maidens dancing at the crossroads described in de Valera's 1943 St Patrick's Day broadcast were chaste, young ones. Knowing the family's vulnerability, Kate redoubles her vigilance. She's aghast at Jack's participation in Ryangan festivals that 'aren't Christian ceremonies' (BF, p. 47/McG, p. 59); polygamy, she reminds them, is 'not what Pope Pius XI considers to be the holy sacrament of matrimony' (BF, p. 63); Saint Nina is not in her prayerbook (BF, p. 19). Obsessed with her family's reputation, Kate recognizes what a liability their sexuality is and how risky loving men, even as sons or brothers, can be. Her dispensation of love and authority, which Seamus Deane identifies as Friel's 'one elusive theme',[18] sometimes confuses even her.

Michael's illegitimacy was a reality that was not unknown in Ireland in 1936. The non-marital birth rate in the Free State was 2.6% of all births in 1921–23. 'From there,' notes J. H. Whyte, 'the figure crept upward till it reached a momentary peak of 3.5 per cent in 1933–4.'[19] After the war, it rose to 3.9% and then fell to 1.6%. By 1969, it had risen only to 2.6%. Jack speaks of Michael as 'a love child' and expresses his wish that all the sisters might have love children. In one of his anthropological moments, Jack shocks Kate in his report of the Ryangan view of non-marital children: 'In Ryanga women are eager to have love-children. The more love-children you have, the more fortunate the household is thought to be' (BF, p. 41). In Ireland, as Arensberg and Kimball report, the antithetical opinion prevailed: 'Apart from the moral censure misconduct brings upon a young woman and the shame it [giving birth to a non-marital child] inflicts upon the people of her "name", it brings as well the destruction of her social role.'[40] Typically, unmarried mothers would emigrate or be sent to a home, such as the Magdalen laundries depicted in Patricia Burke Brogan's *Eclipsed* (1991). What would have been extremely unusual is for Michael to be raised by a single mother in the home with neither apology nor subterfuge. When the play premièred in 1990, 10% of the children born in Ireland were non-marital births; by the time the film appeared it was 18% and by 2001 over 40%. By showing that non-marital births were always a reality in Irish society, glimpsed in Juno's departure with Mary at the end of O'Casey's *Juno and the Paycock* (1926) and in the eponym's parentage in Teresa Deevy's *Katie Roche* (1936), Friel strengthens the bond between the Mundys and his contemporary audience.

In 1936, as in 1990, the world outside Ireland often meant emigration. The Mundy sisters are recurrently linked to friends who have since emigrated. Kate reports meeting Bernie O'Donnell, Maggie's friend, who left Ballybeg for London ('First time back in twenty years' [BF, p. 18]); Maggie's one-time beau, Brian McGuinness, in the play (it is Kate's one-time beau Curly McDaid in the film) emigrated to Australia. The emigration of Rose and Agnes combines self-sacrifice to preserve the family and self-assertion. Like most of Friel's plays, *Dancing at Lughnasa* ends with the dispersal of the family through emigration. *Philadelphia, Here I Come!* depicts the last of Gar's days in Ireland. In *Crystal and Fox* (1969), after Papa's death and Gabriel's arrest, Fox drives Crystal off with the lie that he turned Gabriel in to the police. The metonymic *The Gentle Island* (1971) is left with only two residents. After Commandant Butler's suicide in *Living Quarters* (1977), his family leaves Ireland: Ben goes to Scotland; Anna to America; Helen and Tina to London, where they will rarely see each other. In *Faith Healer* (1979), Grace and Teddy also spend their final days in isolation only blocks away from each other in London. *Translations* (1980) ends with Hugh's sons leaving Ballybeg. After the parable of the 'crazy scheme' to relocate two badgers, *Molly Sweeney* (1995) ends with Frank's departure for Africa, Dr Rice's return to New York City and Molly's institutionalization.

The well-documented demographic anomalies in Ireland concerning emigration are inextricably linked to those of fertility and marriage – all of which 'present features which are unique among civilised peoples'.[41] In spite of the highest birth-rate in Europe, Ireland declined in population in every census between 1841 and 1946 (and, with the exceptions of 1951 and 1966, in every census until the 1990s). The declining population was due mainly to emigration and postponed marriage (or 'celibacy'), which especially in rural areas arose from the pervasive familism described by Arensberg in *The Irish Countryman* (1937). In the familistic model, one son would inherit the land and one daughter would be dowered into marriage; the others might join a religious order or emigrate, but the family could not provide for them. In 1936, 67% of women and 89% of men aged 25–29 in rural Ireland were unmarried. While the fact that all of the Mundy sisters are unmarried is not unusual, other features of family formation in *Dancing at Lughnasa* clearly are. The marriage of the fifteen-year-old Sophia to a sixteen-year-old boy would have been highly unusual in 1936. The film's scene of Rose and Agnes's departure suggests an inclusive sense of the family's formation as Agnes tosses holy water and names each of the remaining six (including Gerry).

Emigration among Irish women was high, in part because females spent more years in formal schooling and frequently might more readily qualify for 'safer' or more respectable positions (such as domestic service). Between 1871 and 1971, female emigration exceeded male emigration in six of ten decades and, as Pauric Travers observes, 'For the century as a whole [i.e. 1871–1971], the annual average emigration for males was 15,707 whereas for females it was 15,983.'[42] Perhaps the most astonishing feature of female emigration is seen in comparison with other European populations. Joseph Lee notes that, 'Whereas European emigration as a whole was predominantly male, with a roughly 2:1 male preponderance, Irish emigration hovered around the 50:50 mark'.[43]

The variety of schemes proposed to curtail emigration testifies to the gravity and persistence of the problem. Early in the century, the nationalistic press attempted to shame emigrants, attributing to them unpatriotic, selfish and frivolous motives. In its application for a patent, the Abbey Theatre argued that it would deter emigration. A Father O'Leary in Cork proposed a marriage bonus for young people (up to £1,500 for a man of 21). De Valera considered plans to build dower (i.e. second) houses on farms to accommodate a son's family in a dwelling separate from that of his parents. After World War II, James Dillon proposed restrictions on emigrants who could not prove 'that they were proceeding to relatives'.[44] As late as 1965, the Catholic bishops asked Taoiseach Sean Lemass to restrict emigration of the under-18s.[45] When Friel was writing *Dancing at Lughnasa*, emigration remained epidemic. Fintan O'Toole notes that '1 in every 12 people living in the Republic in 1982 (i.e. 289,000 people) had emigrated by 1989'.[46]

While documented by a strong statistical record, emigration has implications and consequences that are not easily quantified. The emotional losses and psychological wounds, to both emigrants and the relatives and friends they left behind, are, as Lee argues, compellingly documented in Irish literature.

It is [the writers], some themselves emigrants, who best convey the fetid atmosphere of the forties and fifties, the sense of pervasive, brooding hopelessness at home, the emptiness, the uncomprehending remorse, the heartbreak and heroism of many caught in the web of the 'experience of abandonment' as families were sundered and communities withered.[47]

In the twentieth century, works as diverse as Máirtín Ó Cadháin's 'The Year 1912', Tom Murphy's *A Whistle in the Dark* (1960) and Greg Delanty's 'American Wake' (1995) examine the emotional costs of emigration. For recent generations, emigration has not carried the finality of separation that Ó Cadháin describes in an Aran mother sending her daughter off to America, but assumes larger, metaphoric meanings. Christopher Murray argues that 'both Murphy and Friel were more concerned to view emigration, whatever its causes, as a metaphysical condition affecting the new generation'.[48] In describing emigration in Tom Murphy's plays, Nicholas Grene writes that 'emigration . . . is more than a socio-economic problem; it is the symptom of a psychological malaise not to be relieved by mere material prosperity'.[49]

The emigration of Rose and Agnes is especially painful because they 'vanished without trace' (BF, p. 60/McG, p. 99). Moreover, Michael's narration in the play, drastically abbreviated in the film, describes their plight:

> The scraps of information I gathered about their lives during those missing years were too sparse to be coherent. They moved around a lot. They had worked as cleaners in public toilets, in factories, in the Underground. Then, when Rose could no longer get work, Agnes tried to support them both – but couldn't. From then on, I gathered, they gave up. They took to drink; slept in parks, in doorways, on the Thames Embankment. Then Agnes died of exposure. And two days after I found Rose in that grim hospice – she didn't recognize me, of course – she died in her sleep. (BF, p. 60)

It is not only unhappiness and perhaps not even economic hardship that drives Rose and Agnes away. The threat posed by Danny Bradley is not less than the threat of poverty, even if Robert Welch's reading that Rose 'is raped',[50] presumably on the excursion to Lough Anna, is improbable. Characters often speak of the more generalized desire to 'go away'. For Rose this may mean eloping to America with Danny. For Jack, it is his desire to return to Africa and, on another level, his anticipation of death; for Gerry, Spain; for Michael, manhood; for Rose and Agnes, it is finally a life of drudgery in London. Their reasons for wanting to leave are varied. For Gerry, at least as expressed in the film, it is the need to 'do something', which his careers as dance instructor and travelling salesman, let alone as a partner or parent, cannot accommodate. In the film, Gerry seeks and receives Chris's approval.

> CHRISTINA: Why exactly are you going to Spain, Gerry?
> GERRY: Because I want to do something. I want to do anything. With my life. I have to.
> CHRISTINA: Then do it.
>
> (McG, p. 38)

Similarly, Rose's and Agnes's departure, like that of Danny Bradley's wife, is a risky escape.

Friel's recurrent mythical Donegal town is here, as in his other plays, rife with gossip, menace, violence and malice. Geographically, the Mundys live two miles outside Ballybeg, whose residents populate *Philadelphia, Aristocrats, Translations, Lovers* and *Dancing at Lughnasa.* Friel sets *Wonderful Tennessee* and *Living Quarters* on the periphery of Ballybeg. Often Friel's characters are outsiders to the Ballybeg community. In *The Loves of Cass McGuire,* the title character is a returned émigré; itinerant performers are the principal characters in *Faith Healer* and *Crystal and Fox*; tourists dominate *Wonderful Tennessee* and *The Gentle Island*; Commandant Butler, an Irish army officer, is posted near Ballybeg and, like the characters in *Molly*

19

Sweeney, is not native to it. In *Faith Healer*, Teddy describes the Ballybeg natives who murdered Frank as 'those bloody Irish Apaches'.[51] Welcoming home a mysteriously transformed brother, themselves unmarried, the Mundys are more threatened than nurtured by their community. As a community that might support or sustain the Mundys, Ballybeg fails comprehensively in *Dancing at Lughnasa*.

Father Jack is plainly an outsider, but all of the Mundys live in an uneasy relationship to Ballybeg. 'Why have you no friends?' Kate asks Michael. The family's isolation from (and in) rural Ireland is mitigated by the radio, which brings into the home not only music, but also an array of exotic, international references into their everyday vocabularies. Even the 'slow' Rose knows that Abyssinia is in Africa. Gerry, a Welshman with an Irish child, will go off to fight in Spain. Jack, 'the Irish outcast', spent most of his life in a leper colony in Uganda. The lyrics to 'Anything Goes' (1934), written by a cosmopolitan from Peru, Indiana, waft through the Donegal landscape. In Maeve Binchy's formulation, 'they are perched on the side of a hill in Co. Donegal in 1936, five women alone against the world'.[52] Although many commentators foreground Ireland's isolationism in the 1930s, the perspective in *Dancing at Lughnasa* is more global than parochial.

2

PLAY/SCREENPLAY/FILM

The press materials for the film of *Dancing at Lughnasa* note that Friel had 'no interest in film-making'. Having cultivated non-naturalistic techniques unique to theatre throughout his career, he might well have suspected how rarely his dramatic strategies could survive the transition to film.[53] Friel's involvement in the premières of his plays, including that of *Dancing at Lughnasa*, is to deliver a complete script and to see it staged exactly as written. His presence throughout rehearsals of the first production asserts an uncompromising authorial control: 'As far as I'm concerned, there is a final and complete orchestra score. All I want is musicians to play it. I'm not going to rewrite the second movement for the sake of the oboe player'.[54] For all his reservations about language, he sees the integrity of his texts, stage directions as well as dialogue, as non-negotiable. Dismissive of improvisational and workshop techniques, Friel is the rare contemporary playwright to challenge the stature of the theatre director.[55] In 1991, he told John Lahr:

> Rule number one [for a playwright's artistic survival] would be to not be associated with institutions or directors. I don't want a tandem to develop. Institutions are inclined to enforce characteristics, impose an attitude or a voice or a response. I think you're better to keep away from all of them. It's for that reason that I didn't give *Dancing at Lughnasa* to Field Day to produce.[56]

Friel's desire to control productions of his work led to his directorial début at the age of 65, when he oversaw the première of *Molly Sweeney* at the Gate (transferring to the Almeida in London) in 1994. He has since directed a different cast in *Molly Sweeney* on

21

Broadway in 1996 and *Give Me Your Answer, Do!* at the Abbey in 1997.

The only other Friel play adapted for the screen is *Philadelphia, Here I Come!*, which was directed by John Quested in 1975 and for which Friel did the screenplay. The film featured several members of the original stage cast, including Éamon Kelly as S. B. O'Donnell, Gar's father. Rather than resorting to a voice-over for Gar Private, the film casts Donal McCann as Gar Public and Des Cave as Gar Private. Shot in black and white and running only 95 minutes, the film version of *Philadelphia* is an engaging adaptation that successfully captures the contrast between the emotional reticence of family and community and the turbulence of Gar's interior life. In the 1990s the film adaptation of *Philadelphia* might well have had a niche as an independent production, but in 1975 it did not even find a distributor in North America.

The chairman of the Abbey when Friel's play premièred in 1990, Noel Pearson, who also produced the film in 1998, provides a crucial link between the stage and screen versions. Pearson envisioned *Dancing at Lughnasa* as a film from the outset. Before the New York opening, Pearson tried to secure the option for the film rights and suggested that Friel might do the screenplay. Friel responded that, even if he did the screenplay, the moment it left his hands he would 'automatically forfeit *all* aesthetic rights [his emphasis] . . . Either way I will not have been part of the whole thing. Given that situation I really don't care who does the screenplay . . . My crude intention is to sell the film rights to the highest bidder and forget the whole thing'.[57]

Dancing at Lughnasa is Pat O'Connor's sixth film adaptation of an Irish author, placing Friel in the company of William Trevor (*The Ballroom of Romance* [1980] and *Fools of Fortune* [1990]), Neil Jordan (*Night in Tunisia* [1983]), Bernard MacLaverty (*Cal* [1984]) and Maeve Binchy (*Circle of Friends* [1995]). Taken together, O'Connor's films chronicle Irish life from the 1920s through to the 1980s. *The Ballroom of Romance* offers the strongest comparison with *Dancing at Lughnasa*.

Plate 3. Pat O'Connor

Adapted for television by Trevor, O'Connor's *The Ballroom of Romance*, which won a BAFTA award in 1981, deals with a 35-year-old woman's evening out at a rural ballroom in the 1950s. The television film is rooted in a grim fatalism: Bridie's father's lament, 'It is what God sends us', resurfaces in the words of her friend Eenie: 'You can't change the way things are, Bridie'.[58] In its opening sequences, Bridie (Brenda Fricker) and her crippled father work in muddy fields as the rain pours down. As Bridie, now wearing a striking red dress, arrives at the ballroom, O'Connor evokes the famed shot in Ford's *The Searchers* (1956) as the camera looks out through the ballroom's gloom to the still sunlit exterior. In the ballroom's darkness a banner proclaims 'Happy Homes for Ireland and for God' (borrowed from a dance hall of O'Connor's youth), but there is little happiness here. Bridie's only prospects are the band's drummer, who will marry his landlady, and the drunken hill bachelor, Bowser Egan, away from his aged mother for one of his forays to the pub and ballroom. Near the end of the dance, Mr Dwyer (Cyril Cusack), who presides over a ballroom that endorses rather than subverts rural Irish familism, announces the impending marriages of and recent births to former patrons. Luke Gibbons argues that O'Connor's *The Ballroom of Romance* 'provided a focus for the reassuring belief that the fifties were no longer with us . . . Viewers could confront the harsh realities of poverty, emigration, sexual repression and the enforced domestication of women, secure in the knowledge that "The factory was coming to town" – a recurrent topic of conversation between characters in the play [*sic*] – which would make all these features of the old social order redundant'.[59] *The Ballroom of Romance*, however, graphically realizes what the film of *Dancing at Lughnasa* does not: the gruelling labour in the fields, hopeless frustrations of the ballroom, the sorry truth of diminished possibilities.

In 1997, with O'Connor in place to direct, Pearson arranged for Frank McGuinness to write the screenplay. McGuinness has acknowledged his debt to Friel on several occasions, including an appreciative essay on *Faith Healer* in 1999.[60] In his directorial début, McGuinness revived Friel's *The Gentle Island* at the Abbey's Peacock Theatre in 1988. Both raised as Catholics in Donegal, Friel and McGuinness place greater emphasis on human costs than geo-political events in their interrogations of sectarian conflict. Both, too, have staged the punishing realities of women working outside the home – McGuinness in *Factory Girls* (1982) and Friel in *The Loves of Cass McGuire*. Dramaturgically, both bear the mark of Beckett in rejecting the plot-driven formulations of realistic drama and, instead, creating theatre from largely static situations (three prisoners chained to the wall in the case of *Someone Who'll Watch Over Me* [1992]). Like Friel in *Molly Sweeney* and *Faith Healer*, and perhaps liberated by him, McGuinness accesses character through monologue in 'The Breadman' (1990) and 'Baglady' (1985). McGuinness's most memorable exploration of Frielian non-realistic techniques, specifically direct address, is in *Observe the Sons of Ulster Marching*

Towards the Somme (1986), where the narrator, Old Pyper, is split from his younger incarnation. Like Gar Private and Gar Public in *Philadelphia*, two actors play Young Pyper and Old Pyper.

Plate 4. The Ballroom of Romance

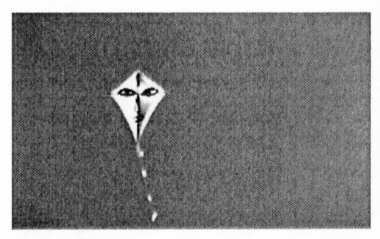

Plate 5.   Credit sequence

Manipulating time and space, the non-naturalistic techniques of McGuinness and Friel are balanced by extremely adept, psychologically credible characterizations. Whereas surrealistic, absurdist or symbolist playwrights rarely create convincing characters or naturalistic dialogue, Friel and McGuinness offer both. Their non-naturalistic techniques counterpoint and sometimes subvert realism. Their characters, moreover, forge rituals, often joyous (and occasionally silly), to compensate for the desiccated ceremonies of lost faiths.

McGuinness's screenplay establishes Michael's physical presence as a child, relocates the sisters's dance near the very end of the film and, by eliminating the period between Friel's acts (when Gerry leaves and returns), provides a continuous linear chronology. Although the screenplay indicates the passage of a week (McG, p. 63) immediately before the sequence in which the sisters examine the photograph album, the film's chronology seems unbroken over several days. The film opens up the setting by moving outside the Mundy home to reveal the landscape and Ballybeg town. In this regard, the adaptation is robust: the number of speaking characters nearly doubles; the filming locales include Lough Anna, the Lughnasa fires, Kate's school and Ballybeg town. In each of these locales, a more sinister view of the Donegal community emerges, one whose minatory powers only hover off stage. Not only does the film 'open up' the play by moving away from the cottage and its garden, but it also achieves this by presenting characters in isolation or in intimate exchanges (between Michael and Gerry, Gerry and Chris, Rose and Agnes, Maggie and Jack). Some of the film's most revealing scenes are set at night. The screenplay develops the male characters, particularly Father Jack, whose presence dominates the early sequences of the film. The camera's focus on Michael as a child during the voice-overs, like Gerry's presence, incorporates the men into the unconventional family formation. The film is especially effective in portraying the dangers of Rose's relationship with Danny Bradley, who never appears on stage but shows up in both of the sequences in Ballybeg, with Rose at Lough Anna and at the Lughnasa fires.

The film's opening credits play over a series of monochromatic stills of the ceremonies marking Jack's departure from Ryanga. Not only will Jack's Ryangan mask and the plumed tricorn link Ballybeg to Africa, so too will the ritualistic dancing and the Lughnasa fires. The kite, 'grotesquely decorated by a child's hand' (McG, p. 5), against a crystalline blue sky advances the linkage of Ireland and Africa. When Michael trips and loses his hold, the kite flies away. Like the hat in the Coen Brothers' *Miller's Crossing* (1990) or the plastic bag in Sam Mendes' *American Beauty* (1999), the windblown kite is an emblem of mutability. And, like the uncontrollable radio, the drifting kite suggests imminent and irrevocable change.

After a brief prelude at the cottage, a telephoto shot shows the family walking to Ballybeg to meet Jack. Like *Translations, Dancing at Lughnasa* depicts a Mediterranean Ireland.[61] O'Connor's film presents a landscape dominated by summer hues, but one that has lost much of the heat of Friel's play. The women wear coats and hats when they venture into Ballybeg, for instance. Aside from the road, the landscape reveals no hint of human habitation: no demarcated or cultivated fields, no houses, vehicles, structures, walls or even livestock. The practical explanation for the unspoiled landscape is that the film was shot in Wicklow at the Kilruddery Estate, on lands under the protection of the Forestry Commission. (To shoot in Donegal would have necessitated per diem and other expenses for cast and crew and would have cost, by Pearson's estimate, an extra million dollars.[62]) Whereas the play and screenplay stress work – the harvesting as well as the women's domestic labour – the film provides only glimpses of any human activity in the countryside. In the screenplay, for instance, 'Everywhere there are signs of harvest time, people working in fields' (McG, p. 34) and 'people working on the bog' (McG, p. 44). In the final cut, however, the work of the harvest

Plate 6.   Rose and Danny on Lough Anna

is confined to two brief sequences: first, when Gerry travels to the Mundy cottage and, second, when Kate pauses "on returning from her second trip into Ballybeg" to greet some men cutting turf. Combined, the two scenes run under thirty seconds. *Dancing at Lughnasa* represents what John Hill, writing about *The Quiet Man* (1952), describes as 'the traditional primitivist view of nature, and particularly wild, unsubdued landscape [that] represents a more profound and permanent reality than the fleeting world of social appearances'.[63] Searching for Rose, Agnes moves through ruins, a reminder of how ancient this idyll is and how deeply romanticized it is on film. The film's landscape is a display of undisturbed natural beauty, unsullied by the labour seen at the opening of *The Ballroom of Romance*. Through epic aerial tracking shots, the extended lyrical explorations of the landscape are facilitated by the motorbike that transports Gerry, and later Chris and Michael, through the countryside. As Chris and Gerry move through hills to the privacy of an isolated glen, the landscape appears untouched. Later, some sheep appear so that Gerry might ask Michael if they're really unicorns, but the film is at pains to depict a pristine world. This was precisely the image Bord Fáilte cultivated for the tourist's gaze. As the artist Robert Ballagh lamented, in such an idealized landscape 'you won't see a car from one end of the day to the other: it's almost as if [Bord Fáilte is] advertising a country nobody lives in'.[64]

As the film moves towards its crisis on the night that Rose and Jack meet at the Lughnasa fires, the landscape is seen in greater detail: first, in the blackberry-gathering excursion and, later, in the climactic sequences at Lough Anna and at the Lughnasa fires. The rugged landscape again dwarfs the individuals who inhabit it. When Danny and Rose are out on Lough Anna, the camera stands well away from them, showing the boat slowly moving across the lake with mountains and the sky looming above them. The intrusion of the cosmopolitan into the Arcadian, what Martin McLoone identifies as 'a key opposition between "tradition" and "modernity"',[65] is best seen in Agnes's dance with Gerry. In a sequence crosscut with the boating sequence, Gerry says 'Pretty milkmaid, put down your pails and dance' (McG, p. 76), and they dance to his *a cappella* rendition of 'Anything Goes'.

In the expansive vistas at Lough Anna and the search for Rose, the landscape's beauty gives way to its potential terror: Danny menaces Rose, the Lughnasa fires lure Jack away from Michael's protective eye, the fox is in the hen house, Kate tells Maggie that she's been fired (McG, p. 85), the sisters cannot find Rose. The accelerated editing pace and quickening soundtrack establishes the ominous atmosphere for the Lughnasa fires, a scene of mayhem, drunken confusion and dancing. Men attired with the headgear of strawboys play bodhrans and leap through the fire. But what fuels Jack's confused enjoyment terrifies Rose.

> JACK: Obi – Obi – Obi – Obi – Obi –
> ROSE: Jack, I want to go home.
> JACK: Are these our relations, Rose? Is this your wedding?
> ROSE: They're savages. Pagans. They're no connection to us.
>
> (McG, p. 86)

As Rose and Jack return to the cottage at daybreak, the terror associated with the landscape vanishes with the dawn. Fraught with danger as well as beauty, this landscape might have existed in a remote past, at any time before industrialization.

On one level, the film's treatment of landscape is consonant with the isolation of the Mundys. The film's visualization of Ballybeg underscores the Mundys' status as outsiders. Meeting Jack in the town, the sisters are configured together, lined up and set apart from the villagers rather than interacting with people they have known all their lives. Unlike the townsfolk, they are well-dressed for Jack's return. They exchange only cursory formalities until a woman chemist steps out to speak with Kate. Knowing the chemist's vitriolic subtext, that Jack is a source of pride but Michael a source of shame, Kate is anxious to extricate herself from the conversation.

The film introduces Rose's 'slowness' in her failure to internalize the regulation of language and action. When first Rose catches sight of Danny Bradley while waiting for Jack's bus, she blurts out his name and starts to move towards him. Agnes gently restrains her and all of her sisters remind Rose of his worthlessness. Maggie and Agnes hem her in, restricting her sight of and movement towards Danny. Father Carlin, too, has come to meet the bus, but he doesn't speak to any of the Mundys. Father Carlin's every suspicion about Jack's 'going native' is confirmed when Jack's case spills open to reveal the mask and hat from Ryanga. Framed out of focus behind Kate and Jack, Father Carlin's presence exudes menace. As consoling as the landscape might be to the film's audience, it does little to assuage Jack's confusion. Stepping off the bus, Jack recognizes neither his sisters nor the town (McG, p. 13). Even after Kate assures him that he is home in Ireland, he recoils in grief: 'Mother is dead. She's not here. She's dead' (McG, p. 13).

On her second, even more hellish, trip into Ballybeg, Kate hears only bad news: Mrs McLoughlin's news of the knitting factory that will end Rose and Agnes's meagre income; Sophia's barbed enquiry about the Harvest Ball; Danny Bradley's assertion that he has no wife. Like her earlier conversation with the chemist, these conversations are steeped in malice. Her biting comments about Danny's wife ('All kinds of things can happen to a body in England. They're not respectable people there as we are in Ballybeg' [McG, p. 40]) are as facetious as Sophia's questions. These laden exchanges anticipate Kate's more intimidating meeting with Father Carlin at her school. As he paces at the back of the classroom, Father Carlin stands in a position of complete power and panoptic knowledge. Of Father Jack, a man he has never met, Carlin says 'I know everything about him' (McG, p. 43). Carlin controls the conversation with Kate, challenging her every statement and finishing her sentences for her.

Mediating between the hostility of Ballybeg and the beauty and terror of the landscape is the Mundy cottage. Immaculately maintained, the cottage is more the site of de Valera's frugal comfort than of rural poverty. The flowers that adorn the windowsills are matched by the care the sisters devote to their appearance. The cottage is also the location for music as broadcast by the radio. The impact of radio figured in other films from the 1980s, including Woody Allen's *Radio Days* (1987) and Bob Clark's *A Christmas Story* (1983). Like *Dancing at Lughnasa*, both films are narrated by an adult who recalls the transformation of his childhood wrought by this wondrous technology. In the former, the radio unites the country during World War II, not only in concern over the war, but also in the enjoyment of music (conga lines snake through Brooklyn apartments) and in the sorrow over a child's death. In Ireland, argues Christine Hunt Mahony, radio had a comparable effect: 'Radio Éireann had a far greater unifying effect on Irish listeners than print media had ever had on Irish readers.'[66] Here the radio draws the family together, as when it lures Jack from the isolation of his bedroom.

In Friel's play, the radio's unpredictability serves dramaturgical purposes by creating both music and silence. The radio's magical powers facilitate transitions, interrupt routines, motivate entrances and provide diversions. Its propensity to disrupt the action with a burst of music and to conk out just as suddenly reminds us that the Mundys do not control technology; technology, in fact, has its own powers over them. The very presence of radio in the Mundy cottage offers ambivalent consequences: it provides sporadic pleasure (and on stage triggers the frenzied dance of the sisters), but also emblematizes the encroaching industrialization and modernization, the 'progress' that will end their way of life. Especially in the film version, radio is linked with other new technologies – the knitting factory, Gerry's phonographs and motorbike – that bring the industrial revolution to Ballybeg.

When the diegetic music first draws Jack into his sisters' company, he pronounces the radio a miracle. But Kate corrects him: 'It's no miracle, Jack. It's science' (McG, p. 20). Miracles, as far as Kate is

Plate 7.　*Radio Days*

concerned, emanate only from God, specifically a Roman Catholic one. Rose offers a third alternative: 'It's not science, Kate. It's the god of Lughnasa' (McG, p. 20). Here, as throughout the screenplay and film, the tensions within the family – including numerous instances when the younger sisters challenge and defy Kate's authority – are even more evident than in the stage play. After Kate announces that they will all sleep in their own beds, meaning that neither Michael nor Chris will sleep with Gerry in the barn, Chris overrides Kate's decision saying she'll read to Michael: 'And that too, Kate, is final' (McG, p. 60). As she does in the play, Agnes calls Kate 'a damned righteous bitch' and defends herself and Rose: 'What you have here, Kate, are two unpaid servants' (BF, p. 34/McG, p. 55). When Kate insists that Rose's disappearance be kept a secret, Maggie says she'll seek help from Gerry. These tensions, however, are at least momentarily resolved in the film by the sisters' dance.

Plate 8.   Uncle Jack in bedroom

McGuinness's script is extremely effective in opening up the private, nocturnal lives of the characters. Agnes watches Chris sneak out to the barn to sleep with Gerry. Alone in their room, Agnes asks Rose 'Do you ever want to go away, Rose? . . . Just wanted . . . away?' (McG, pp. 61–62). When Rose confides her plans to meet Danny Bradley, Agnes suggests another departure that becomes 'Our big secret' (McG, p. 62). Seen in his bedroom struggling with an unfamiliar environment where even roses and roosters are strange, Jack inhabits a liminal state that Kate dismisses as 'dreaming' or as 'daft'. Rather than growing stronger, as he does in the play, Jack appears increasingly detached from his family and environment in the film. His uneasiness with the English language and with what is now his home produces his anthropological assessments of the unfamiliar: Rose's pet rooster is 'a strange white bird on my window-sill' (McG, p. 51); the Feast of the Assumption becomes 'the goddess rising through the sky and the stars to greet her son' (McG, p. 20). Not only does Jack recall African ceremonies, but he finds cognates all around him. Having seen the power of other faiths, as when a medicine man cured a priest addicted to quinine, Jack no longer accepts that salvation is possible only through One True Church.

In the film's access to Jack's contemplative moments, another pattern of departure emerges. One of the screenplay's many omens is Jack telling Maggie 'I think I have come home to die' (McG, p. 25). In the second half of the film, the images and omens of departure build. As he taps out a rhythm on a bucket and shuffles a crude dance, Jack says: 'Okawa, I'm coming home' (a line that appears in the film, but in neither screenplay nor play). The time of Gerry's departure grows near. Rose and Agnes speak of their secret. Jack tells Gerry he may return to Africa. Agnes turns off 'The Homes of Donegal' saying 'I can't stick this song' (McG, p. 97). Rose doesn't want another rooster (McG, p. 97). With the soundtrack swelling, Michael recalls 'waiting to become a man. Waiting to get – to get away' (McG, p. 101).

In the face of the imminent dispersal of the family, the film presents the sisters' dance as a joyous, if elegiac, celebration. Rose joins Maggie; then Agnes and Chris. Kate cowers, book in hand, until she, too, joins in and leads her sisters outside. They dance together as the men – Gerry, Jack and, finally, Michael – look on, dumbfounded by this spontaneous outburst. The sisters all know the steps and, for once, even Kate allows herself a moment of pleasure. Whereas McGuinness's script incorporates Friel's stage directions (the 'defiance . . . wild roar . . . a mood of near hysteria . . . the music stops abruptly in mid-phrase' [BF, pp. 21–22/McG, pp. 92–93]), none of these elements made the final cut. In the film, polite whoops replace roars. All of the sisters smile throughout their dance. With all their quarrels, secrets and unhappiness held in abeyance, the sequence provides a final happy moment in the film and in the life of the family. The camera pans round to each of the sisters, again isolated, exhausted, panting for breath, standing stock still in the garden, but without the shame seen after their dance on stage. The film's dance is, like the women's work, beautiful – its disturbing abject

Plate 9.   Maggie and Chris in mirror

elements purged. Rather than employing 'The Mason's Apron' or the 'very fast raucous music' of the screenplay, Whelan's composition is restrained, subdued by a lush orchestration with strings. Likewise, in the film's depiction of the exchange of hats, Jack's British army uniform is not a soiled, crumpled remnant of the past. On the contrary, Jack looks quite dapper. Similarly, the work of the sisters – washing, sweeping, chopping – is aestheticized in two montage sequences that stress the rhythms rather than the drudgery of work. Whereas Friel's stage directions specify that 'the clothes of all the sisters reflect their lean circumstance' (BF, n.p. 2 before 1), in the film they wear stylish if modest period costumes. The wardrobe and choreography run counter to Friel's very explicit stage directions and advance the film's aestheticization of the women.

The film's dance is revisited as the visual image that accompanies Michael's closing narration. The narration is more succinct and euphemistic in describing the dispersal of the family and the fate of Rose and Agnes. Entirely omitted from the final narration is the fact that Gerry never made good on his promise to buy his son a bicycle, as well as any reference to Gerry's marriage and family in Wales. The reprise of the aerial shot of the sisters dancing together is followed by a return to the opening sequence, where Michael chases after a kite, and, finally, Dolores Keane's reprising 'Down by the Salley Gardens'. The repetitions memorialize the women's happiness, minimize their misery and suggest that these moments can be accessed at any time.

Whereas McGuinness's screenplay is extraordinarily faithful to Friel's play, the film departs in crucial ways. The film incorporates lines authored by neither Friel nor McGuinness that express Michael's uncritical nostalgia for his childhood. In voice-over narration, for instance, the adult Michael says, 'That lovely summer I thought would never end. We laughed and played to our hearts' content. And I was king of the castle surrounded by all who loved me.' This sentimentality is unmatched by anything in the play or screenplay. Not only does it impute adult emotions to the child, but it also establishes this summer as a lost, idyllic moment and thereby provides the basis for transforming the sisters' dance from transgressive to triumphal.

3

MUSIC AND DANCE

Dance, like the cracked looking-glass in which Chris and Maggie examine themselves, is one of the central tropes of Irish expression. In the twentieth century, even Irish politicians employed images of dance to evoke their image of Ireland. De Valera's 'happy maidens' conveyed an image of feminine beauty and chastity in an idyllic land. In her inaugural speech as President in 1990, Mary Robinson hoped that 'I the President can sing to you, citizens of Ireland, the joyous refrain of the fourteenth-century Irish poet as recalled by W. B. Yeats: "I am Ireland . . . come dance with me in Ireland."' In Robinson's rhetoric, dance was an inclusive celebration that reached out to a diasporic population. Her invitation not only reflects the title metaphor in *Dancing at Lughnasa* but also rejoins de Valera's vision. The sisters' dance in *Dancing at Lughnasa* is a pivotal dramatic moment in the stage play, the culmination of the film and the most significant difference between play and film. Closely associated with and triggered by music, the dance of the sisters is the central display of the women's physicality, an action intimately associated with ritual – in this instance, the marginalized ritual of the play's title.

Even in his earliest plays, Friel employed music to serve dramaturgical ends. Harry White, in discussing *Philadelphia, Aristocrats* and *Faith Healer,* writes of Friel's use of music as a textual element: 'music enters the text as a decisive agent in both the dramatic structure and emotional meaning of the drama'.[67] Music, like dance, is a liberating alternative to language, expressive when words fail. Mendelssohn articulates what Gar Public cannot: 'D'you know what that music says? (to S. B.) It says that once upon a time a boy and his father sat in a blue boat on a lake . . .'.[68] Typically, Friel uses music to remind characters of otherness: the past, different cultures, other places.

Radio transmissions hastened the end of the isolation of the Mundys, of rural Donegal, of all of Ireland. Friel's own comment is that 'I think what's interesting is that it's music from a different culture that liberates them. They haven't absorbed it into their life and into their culture and tamed it. It's still slightly exotic'.[69] In *Dancing at Lughnasa* the extensive use of diegetic music situates the characters in an Irish as well as an international context at a time when native Irish culture contested with exotic imports. After Independence, writes Martin McLoone, 'a fear of forms of popular culture ("music-hall dope") . . . was a constant refrain in the debates on broadcasting in the Dáil over the next two decades, very often articulated through regrets at the amount of dance music or "jazz" that was played on national radio'.[70] The first music from Marconi heard on stage (but not in the film) is not native Irish culture entering the home, but a reminder of colonialism: 'a sudden, loud three-second blast of "The British Grenadiers"' (BF, p. 4). The film places far greater emphasis on Irish music: Sean MacBride's composition 'The Homes of Donegal', performed by Maighread Ní Dhomhnaill, is broadcast over the radio twice and the sisters sing 'Down by the Salley Gardens' sitting around the kitchen table. The film subordinates the diegetic music to Whelan's soundtrack and underplays the impact of jazz: a brief interlude of Fats Waller's 'I'm More than Satisfied' is barely audible.

Perhaps out of fidelity to his aunts and mother, Friel has none of the Mundy sisters play a musical instrument and only two of them, Rose and Maggie, sing. On stage, their only songs are 'The Isle of Capri' and ditties, one of which trivializes the bombing campaign that deployed conventional and chemical weapons in the fascist annexation of Ethiopia the previous May: 'Mussolini will be there / With his airplanes in the air.' In the film Maggie also sings a composition by McGuinness, 'Gypsy Play Your Violin', that bespeaks the desire for escape and romance.

Dance is perhaps more common in the home than music. Images and instances of impromptu dance suffuse *Dancing at Lughnasa*. Arensberg and Kimball describe spontaneous episodes of dance among unmarried females in rural Ireland: 'Occasionally a dance breaks the ordinary succession of work and evening talk in the kitchen', although those who dance are 'girls . . . the unmarried younger women and adolescents'.[71] Although unmarried, the Mundy sisters are no longer adolescents – they range in age from twenty-six to forty. Arensberg and Kimball associate dance in rural Ireland primarily with communal festivity and with courtship leading to marriage.[72] Rural dances are central to what they describe as the inexorable pattern of familism, the formalized cultural patterns that assure the orderly transferral of property from one generation to the next through marriage and children. But, from its opening moments when Maggie joins Rose's 'gauche, graceless shuffle that defies the rhythm of the song' (BF, p. 3), *Dancing at Lughnasa* employs dance 'as if language had surrendered to movement' (BF, p. 71/McG, p.

Plate 10. Dancing on the road, 1920s, Glendalough

101), expressive, that is, of suppressed subjectivity and sexuality. Rose's immediate response to music is 'to launch into a dance – and the music suddenly dies' (BF, p. 4). Maggie asks, 'Are we all for a big dance somewhere?' (BF, p. 5), and tangoes with her hen bucket to 'The Isle of Capri'. As Gerry remarks, 'Everybody wants to dance' (BF, p. 28).

Dance accommodates and expresses what language cannot. Maggie proposes that dance might even serve Jack when words fail him.

> JACK: Do you know what I found strange? Coming back in the boat there were days when I couldn't remember even the simplest words. Not that anybody seemed to notice. And you can always point, Margaret, can't you?
> MAGGIE: Or make signs.
> JACK: Or make signs.
> MAGGIE: Or dance.
>
> (BF, p. 40)

By 1990, when *Dancing at Lughnasa* premièred at the Abbey, Friel had often spoken of and dramatized the failures of language. In drafting *Dancing at Lughnasa*, he repeatedly noted that language had not only failed, but also specifically 'betrayed' these characters.[72] The ways in which language betrays them are many: Jack's inability to recall words; simple misunderstandings; Rose's occasionally inappropriate repetitions; the gossip that preys upon the Mundys. More vicious are the subtle passive–aggressive betrayals such as the chemist's barbed exchange with Kate at the beginning of the film, which Maggie glosses as 'give him your arse and call it parsley' (McG, p. 11). Similarly, Chris exposes the hostility that Kate masks as chitchat:

> KATE: I have to laugh at you, Christina Mundy.
> CHRISTINA: Whenever you say you have to laugh at me, Kate, I know you're not laughing.
>
> (McG, p. 24)

O'Connor exposes the hypocrisy that language facilitates in cutting directly from an exterior shot in which Mrs McLoughlin tells Kate that she was Sophia's favourite teacher to the interior of Morgan's Arcade, where Sophia calls Kate 'That old bitch the gander' (McG, p. 36). Unlike language, dance cannot readily accommodate such hypocrisy.

The power of language to betray lies in its capacity for irony and deceit. Numerous times Kate tries to silence her sisters: 'No need for corner boy language, Christina' (BF, p. 22); 'I'm not going to have it [Rose's disappearance] broadcast all over' (BF, p. 56); 'This is silly talk' (BF, p. 13); 'And there'll be no more discussion about it' (BF, p. 13); 'Not a word of this must go outside these walls – d'you hear? – not a syllable' (BF, p. 49); 'I wish you wouldn't use words like that, Christina' (BF, p. 69). Kate is especially censorious of Rose: 'I'm shocked and disappointed to hear you repeating rubbish like that, Rose!' (BF, p. 17); 'You've offered us that cheap wisdom already, Rose' (BF, p. 19); 'That's a very unchristian thing to say, Rose' (BF, p. 25); and, when Rose teases her about Austin Morgan, 'For God's sake, Rose, shut up, would you!' (BF, p. 10). Kate's efforts to control the family extend beyond trying to regulate speech. Kate's antipathy to pleasure – Maggie's Wild Woodbines, Chris's love for Gerry, Jack's spirituality, 'the old pagan songs' and dance – emanates from an anxiety about reputation, as if the denial of pleasure enhances the status and viability of the family.

Kate is no more successful in her attempts to regulate dance. She chides her sisters for wanting to dance 'at our time of life' and ultimately vetoes the possibility that they would all attend the Harvest Dance. When Jack asks her to join him in dancing in the film, Kate becomes agitated and rebukes him: 'You are an ordained priest. You do not dance' (McG, p. 22). Jack later defies her when he picks up two sticks and 'begins to beat out a structured beat whose rhythm gives him pleasure . . . JACK begins to shuffle – dance in time to his tattoo . . . as he dances – shuffles, he mutters – sings – makes occasional sounds that are incomprehensible and almost inaudible' (BF, pp. 41–42/cf. McG, p. 57). This, too, disturbs Kate, who guides Jack away on another constitutional walk.

Kate was not the only one intent on regulating speech, pleasure and dance. After Independence, the Church railed against the lax morality associated with drinking, gambling and dancing, especially new dance styles performed to jazz music. Like film and imported newspapers, jazz and dance crazes were pernicious foreign influences abetted by powerful technologies: the radio, the phonograph and the cinema. As Archbishop Gilmartin of Tuam cautioned in 1926:

> In recent years, the dangerous occasions of sin had been multiplied. The old Irish dances had been discarded for foreign importations, which, according to all accounts, lent themselves not so much to rhythm as to low sensuality. The actual hours of sleep had been turned into hours of debasing pleasure. Company-keeping under the stars of night had succeeded in too many places to the good old Irish custom of visiting, chatting and story-telling from one house to another, with the Rosary to bring all home in due time.[74]

Pastoral warnings led to agitation for xenophobic legislation. As in the Censorship of Publications Act (1929), these non-Irish influences were seen as perverting and undermining a native tradition that was, in turn, idealized. Intent on purging degenerate alien influences ('the fleshpots of Egypt'), traditional Irish dance organizations embarked on their own purification and regulation: dance teachers would not only be registered, but Irish-speaking.[75] At the same time, social dancing underwent a commodification that moved it out of private homes, away from the crossroads and into commercial establishments that offered modern music in all-night raves. In Teresa Deevy's 1936 play *Katie Roche*, for instance, the title character anticipates that she will 'be likely to hear the dance music all night'.[76] New dances occasioned physical contact and intimacy between partners that often

Plate 11. Dance scene

left little room for the Holy Ghost. Dance came under state control with the passage of the Public Dance Hall Act in 1935, which required the licensing of all public dances by District Justices. The state regulation of dance halls, however, may have had its own pernicious effect: 'One [clerical] writer complained that it stamped out informal dances in private houses, where the young people danced under the eyes of their elders, and diverted them to commercial dance halls, where there was less supervision'.[77]

For Friel's reviewers and anyone who saw the original production, the sisters's dance was the play's central moment. The diaries Friel kept in May 1989 while writing *Dancing at Lughnasa* describe 'dancing as release and entrance to supposed and almost forgotten truth'.[78] Clearly, those forgotten truths tap elements embodied in the dance: physicality, pleasure, release, transcendence and an expressivity not possible through language. There is considerable tension attached to the moment when Kate refuses to allow her sisters to attend the Harvest Ball: it recalls the fact that the Mundy sisters are ageing (and still unmarried), that Sophia has facetiously enquired as to whether the Mundys would attend this year's dance, that a very narrow decorum prevails. It is specifically Rose's 'bizarre and abandoned dance' (BF, p. 13) that triggers Kate's anxiety and her decisive rejection of the plan:

> KATE: Just look at yourselves! Dancing at our time of day? That's for young people with no duties and no responsibilities and nothing in their head but pleasure.
>
> AGNES: Kate, I think we –
>
> KATE: Do you want the whole countryside to be laughing at us? – women of our years? – mature women, *dancing*? What's come over you all? And this is Father Jack's home – we must never forget that – ever. No, no, we're going to no harvest dance.
>
> (BF, p. 13)

Fearing ridicule, especially ridicule of Rose, Kate is adamant.

Only after the possibility of the sisters participating in the community's dance has been ruled out do they perform the dance of the sisters, midway through the first act of the play but not until the end of the film. Back from shopping, Kate tells Maggie that her old friend Bernie O'Donnell has returned to Ballybeg with fourteen-year-old twin daughters. Usually the joker and purveyor of bad riddles, Maggie is silenced and staggered by the news: 'Maggie goes to the window and looks out so that the others cannot see her face' (BF, p. 19). She repeats her friend's name several times, as if summoning up a field of memories and possibilities. Retreating into the past, Maggie recalls in considerable detail attending a Lughnasa dance with Bernie in Ardstraw twenty-two years earlier. Reminded that Bernie's good fortune might have been hers, Maggie streaks her face with flour and launches into her dance, an alternate discourse that bespeaks jealousy, rage, frustration, desire, creativity and *je m'en fous*. Through dance, she challenges the systematic efforts made to repress, silence, control and immobilize her. In rehearsals for the

Plate 12. Cover of US–DVD

original Abbey production, the five women playing the Mundy sisters prevailed upon Friel and the director Patrick Mason to allow them to develop the dance on their own.[79]

On stage, the music that triggers the dance is 'The Mason's Apron', a piece of céilí music which Friel likens to the 'piece of thumpety-thump' in *Philadelphia*, 'only more anguished and manic. And in both plays the purpose was to explode theatrically the stifling rituals and discretions of family life.'[80] The film uses Whelan's 'Dancing at Lughnasa', plainly not a piece of aul' thumpety-thump, but Irish traditional music overscored in a John Williamsesque arrangement. The choreography in the film, moreover, has none of the abandon that both Friel and McGuinness describe and that was realized in the première production. Instead, the sisters' dance is aptly summed up by one critic as 'a lovely burst of energy that brings them together for a triumphal moment'.[81] Worse, an image not seen in the film was used on the North American video and DVD cases: the women holding hands outdoors, smiling, their eyes raised to heaven.

Dance emphasizes the women's bodies. Their physicality is primarily associated with routine work, especially regimented, repetitive tasks such as knitting, sweeping, ironing, all of which have distinctive rhythms captured on both stage and screen. Dance is the only form of physicality associated with pleasure and, at least for Chris, with sexuality. Quite unlike stepdancing, which is prescriptive, performative and directed outward (towards an audience), the sisters' dance is spontaneous, expressive and individualized. When they dance, they travesty the strict protocols of Irish stepdancing which prescribe the straight arms held firmly against the body to inhibit the movement of the breasts. Maggie's dance is extemporaneous, her 'arms, legs, hair, long bootlaces flying . . . a white-faced frantic dervish' (BF, p. 21). The women scream and flail about. Friel describes Maggie as transformed: 'breathing deeply, rapidly. Now her features become animated by a look of defiance, of aggression; a crude mask of happiness' (BF, p. 21).

Plate 13. Bríd Ní Neachtain, Bríd Brennan, Catherine Byrne and Sorcha Cusack (1990 Abbey Theatre production)

Friel's detailed stage directions emphasize the transgressive nature of their dance, incorporating their desperation and frenzy in the choreography: 'But the movements seem caricatured; and the sound is too loud; and the beat is too fast; and the almost recognizable dance is made grotesque . . .' (BF, p. 21). The stage directions emphasize this as a dangerous, perhaps unique, moment – one seized in partial compensation for not attending the Harvest Ball and for larger missed opportunities: 'there is a sense of order being consciously subverted, of the women consciously and crudely caricaturing themselves, indeed of near-hysteria being induced' (BF, p. 22). Denied the possibility of release and pleasure because of their station, age and sex, the women appropriate their domestic space to enact their frenzied dance. The last to abandon herself to the dance is Kate; her abandon is in proportion to her reserve. The guardian of a rigid decorum and the family's reputation, Kate dances only once. In the play, Kate does not join her sisters, but dances alone, 'totally concentrated, totally private' (BF, p. 22).[82]

But the music stops, literally, as it will figuratively. The moment when the radio stops is something over which the Mundys have no control; it is as uncertain and ungovernable as their future. After the transmission 'stops abruptly in mid-phrase', the women 'look at each other only obliquely; avoid looking at each other; half smile in embarrassment; feel and look slightly ashamed and slightly defiant' (BF, p. 22). Like any form of human expression, dance is not always beautiful. Abashed and ashamed, the women make an uneasy re-entry into the workaday world. Chris's comment about the radio's unpredictability applies equally to their social situation: 'Maybe a valve has gone' (BF, p. 23). The valve, the release mechanism, has indeed gone.

Friel and McGuinness describe the sisters' dance as what Mikhail Bakhtin identifies as the carnivalesque. In the introduction to *Rabelais and His World*, Bakhtin observes that the carnival atmosphere 'pervaded agricultural feasts' such as harvest, of which Lughnasa is one. 'As opposed to the official feast,' he writes, 'one might say that carnival celebrated temporary liberation from the prevailing truth and from the established order; it marked the suspension of all hierarchical rank, privileges, norms, and prohibitions.'[83] Bakhtin focuses on the Christian origin of carnival, the days before Lent when believers bid, as the word's etymology suggests, 'farewell to the flesh' – both to the meat from which they would abstain and to the human flesh they would mortify in hopes of spiritual vivification. Even today, carnival is associated with the revelry of Mardi Gras. To prepare for the dance, Maggie streaks her face with flour. That Chris dons Jack's surplice, which she has been ironing, to join her sisters marks this moment as a travesty of the sacred, as the quintessentially carnivalesque. After the sisters' dance, Kate hastens to restore her regime of denial. She criticizes Rose for wearing wellingtons, Maggie for smoking, Chris for wearing the surplice and Agnes for saving the money that might have taken them to the Harvest Ball. (That money will instead fund Rose's and Agnes's departure from Ballybeg forever.) Later in the act, when Kate watches Chris dance with Gerry and observes that Chris is as beautiful as Bernie, Maggie is again staggered. Friel's stage directions specify that Maggie 'moves slowly away from the window and sits motionless' (BF, p. 33). Maggie again imagines a happier life than might have been her own, but she has danced her last dance.

The film relocates these defiant, aggressive energies to the sequence when Father Jack encounters Rose and Danny Bradley at the Lughnasa bonfires. Here, too, the indulgence of the body (although not the female body) underscores the transgressive elements of dance. These rituals, suppressed because of their orgiastic quality, are dying out – driven off to the 'back hills'. The film departs significantly from Friel's stage play in visualizing what was only reported on stage. Lured by the bonfires, Father Jack wanders off hoping to recapture the ecstatic splendour of the Ryangan ceremonies: 'dancing . . . for days on end!' (BF, p. 48/McG, p. 58). Wearing a garland of red poppies that recalls one of the variant names for Lughnasa, Garland Sunday, Jack asks 'Is this Africa?' (McG, p. 86). The vestigial rituals of Lughnasa may be seen as either degenerate or as driven to excess precisely because they have been marginalized. Bakhtin would see them as purely carnivalesque.

There are, of course, no Ryangans in Africa. By changing two letters of his uncle's African posting, Nyenga, Friel drew upon one of the most common Irish names to depict the universal need for release, ritual and Bakhtin's carnival. That need for release and the incorporation of the pagan point to Friel's strongest classical influence: the last of great Greek tragedians, Euripides. In Athens, the taming and shaping of aggression and excess resulted in the Dionysiac festivals which venerated, through dance and drama, the Greek god of wine and harvest, of nurture and destruction, of physical nature and spiritual ecstasy. Unwilling to reconcile the ways of god to his audience, Euripides interrogates the tenuous human constructs of morality and justice. His best-known works, *Medea*, *Hippolytus* and the *Bacchae*, end not only with predictable parricide, but specifically with filicide for which a parent is responsible. In all three plays, the beloved son's death extinguishes the family line. Friel acknowledged his debt to Euripides in the subtitle of *Living Quarters*: 'after *Hippolytus*'. In *Dancing at Lughnasa*, the linkage with the *Bacchae* is both subtler and more profound. In the *Bacchae*, Dionysus destroys the Thebans who deny his divinity by contriving to have Pentheus's mother and aunts tear Pentheus to pieces in their frenzied, orgiastic revels. Dance becomes murderous, the ultimate assertion of Dionysus's power over mortals. The Mundy sisters neither eviscerate livestock nor murder their son/nephew, but in their dance they experience Dionysiac release and make an awkward return to quotidian existence. After their dance, they, like Euripides's bacchantes, are humiliated, ashamed of their behaviour. Friel situates other outbreaks of Dionysian frenzy in Ballybeg. Frank's murder in *Faith Healer* takes place on 'A Dionysian night. A Bacchanalian night. A frenzied, excessive Irish night when ritual was consciously and relentlessly debauched'.[84] In *Wonderful Tennessee*, the young boy was not simply killed by drunks, but ritually murdered and dismembered by the pilgrims returning from the Eucharistic Congress. Without ritualized release, the community represses such needs and thereby risks such murderous violence. E. R. Dodds's observation on the *Bacchae* has immediate relevance to *Dancing at Lughnasa*:

> The 'moral' of the *Bacchae* is that we ignore at our peril the demand of the human spirit for Dionysiac experience. For those who do not close their minds against it such experience can be a deep source of spiritual power and *eudaimonia* [inner happiness]. But those who repress the demand in themselves or refuse its satisfaction to others transform it by their action

into a power of disintegration and destruction, a blind natural force that swings away the innocent with the guilty.[85]

On stage, the sisters' dance is only a brief moment of carnival and their final farewell to the flesh.

4

NARRATION AND MEMORY

In *The Haunted Stage*, Marvin Carlson describes the centrality of memory, collective and personal, in modern drama. The repetition of familiar patterns – oft-told stories, cultural memories, myths, parables – argues Carlson, is and always has been at the heart of theatre:

> Theatre, as a simulacrum of the cultural and historical process itself, seeking to depict the full range of human actions within their physical context, has always provided society with the most tangible records of its attempts to understand its own operations. It is the repository of cultural memory, but, like the memory of each individual, it is also subject to continual adjustment and modification as the memory is recalled in new circumstances and contexts.[86]

Friel's treatment of memory, closely allied to his treatment of history, candidly admits its subjectivity and selectivity.

Structurally and dramaturgically, Friel's play bears an uncanny resemblance to Tennessee Williams's memory play, *The Glass Menagerie* (1945). As Christopher Murray points out, 'When *Lughnasa* premièred at the Abbey in April 1990, *The Glass Menagerie* was playing in the Peacock, the Abbey's annex, directed by Friel's daughter Judy'.[87] Williams's narrator, Tom Wingfield, describes the decade shared by both plays as:

> That quaint period, the thirties, when the huge middle class of America was matriculating in a school for the blind. Their eyes had failed them, or they had failed their eyes, and so they were having their fingers press forcibly down on the fiery Braille alphabet of a dissolving economy. In Spain there was revolution.[88]

Both plays employ a single domestic set in which new-fangled technologies behave erratically, the radio in Friel's play recalling the enlarged photograph of Tom's long-departed, grinning father that 'lights up' to remind the family (and audience) of his escape. Kate and Amanda believe that only their code of diligent propriety and austerity will deliver them from ruin. In both plays, too, a central episode of dance offers fleeting release, but, as that moment passes, so does the possibility of the dancers' happiness. In *The Glass Menagerie*, dance celebrates Laura's momentary emergence from her emotional shell before the breaking of the glass figurine (the unicorn, like Laura, losing that which makes it unique) precipitates her permanent withdrawal from reality. (There is even mention of a unicorn in *Dancing at Lughnasa*.)

More important than these potentially coincidental similarities – unicorns, erratic appliances, even the Spanish Civil War – is the way in which Friel and Williams treat memory. Williams pointedly describes the unrealistic quality of Tom as narrator: 'The narrator is an undisguised convention of the play. He takes whatever license with dramatic convention as is convenient to his purposes.' Tom describes his dramatic function in terms of another stage metaphor: 'I am the opposite of the stage magician. He gives you illusion that has the appearance of truth. I give you truth in the pleasant disguise of illusion'.[89] Friel's Michael has it both ways: in his memory 'everything is simultaneously actual and illusory' (BF, p. 71). For Friel and Williams (whose given names, Thomas Lanier, suggest his narrator Tom as an authorial persona), a therapeutic motive informs the narrative stance. Williams's sister, like Laura, was unable to cope with life's demands and underwent the psychiatric solution of her day: frontal lobotomy. Grounded in autobiography and subjectivity, *Dancing at Lughnasa*, like *The Glass Menagerie*, rewrites the personal past. As Friel has said: 'The play provides me with an acceptable fiction for them [his aunts] now'.[90]

Friel draws upon or creates stage devices unique to theatre and, in several instances, unique to a particular play. In *Translations*, the governing stage convention is that characters speaking Irish actually speak English, as do those speaking English, although the Anglophones cannot understand the Gaelgeoirí. Extra-dramatic commentators shatter the continuums of time and space and supply multiple readings of the deaths of Lily, Skinner and Michael in *The Freedom of the City*. Only in the course of their monologues does the audience realize that two of the characters in *Faith Healer* are already dead.

Friel employs narrators who break the fourth wall of realistic drama to speak directly to the audience in no fewer than seven plays. In *Philadelphia*, the term 'narrator' can loosely be applied to Gar Private, since his commentaries challenge and qualify the action on stage and are not heard by other characters. In two plays, *Faith Healer* and *Molly Sweeney*, there is no interaction among the characters on stage, only direct address. In *The Freedom of the City*, the multiplicity of narrators subverts their credibility. Not only do their accounts transgress the theatrical fourth wall, but they also presume the authority of public pronouncements, legal judgements, expert opinions. The narrator in *Dancing at Lughnasa* is most closely related to the narrators in the one-act 'Winners' from *Lovers* and Sir in *Living Quarters*. In the former, two detached narrators, 'Commentators . . . in their late fifties and carefully dressed in good dark clothes',[91] sit in chairs at the edge of the stage and read from an 'official' version Joe's and Mag's last day. In *Living Quarters*, Sir carries and consults the Ledger, although, unlike the Commentators, he rarely reads directly from it: 'And in [the characters'] imagination, out of some deep psychic necessity, they have conceived this (*Ledger*) – a complete and detailed record of everything that was said and done that day.'[92] Sir interacts with characters, most notably with Father Tom, but he exists only as a theatrical entity. There are two significant differences between the Commentators and Sir: first, the characters interact with Sir whereas Joe and Mag are closed off from the Commentators; second, Sir is not bound to the Ledger as the Commentators are to their briskly objective accounts. Michael, like the commentators in 'Winners' and *The Freedom of the City*, is removed by time and space from the action he narrates, a distance of which the theatre audience is reminded by having him play himself as a child.

Structurally, Michael is closer to Cass in *The Loves of Cass McGuire* in that both narrate action in which they participate. Cass, like one of Pirandello's six characters, argues with her brother Harry about how her story will be told.

> HARRY: The story has begun, Cass.
>
> CASS: The story begins where I say it begins, and I say it begins with me stuck in the gawddam workhouse! So you can all get the hell outa here!
>
> HARRY: The story begins in the living room of my home, a week after your return to Ireland. This is my living room and we're going to show bit by bit how you came –
>
> CASS: (*looking around set*): Sure! Real nice and cozy! (*Direct to audience*) The home of my brother, Mister Harold McGuire . . .[93]

Yet hers is not a memory play. Removed by neither time nor space, Cass is immersed in otherwise naturalistic action.

These departures from realism, a dramatic style governed by the artificiality of a fourth wall, make Friel's plays expressly theatrical and decidedly non-cinematic. At once playfully inventive and brazenly indifferent to naturalism, Friel's dramaturgy challenges basic assumptions about theatrical reality in particular and reality in general. Non-realistic stage conventions, especially ones that call attention to themselves, raise formalistic questions about theatrical representation and epistemology. Having all the characters in *Translations* speak English, although most of them are 'in reality' speaking Irish, interrogates that 'reality'. Although the convention sounds as if it would baffle any audience, it was never an obstacle, even for inexperienced audiences in remote venues. In fact, the technique corroborates the centrality and multiple meanings of the acts of translation, especially when the audience recognizes the disparity between Lancey's pronouncements and Owen's translations of them at the end of Act One.

The effects of such overtly theatrical strategies are sweeping. They draw an audience in to a collective of shared assumptions and establish a bond between audience and performance. They endow an audience with powers of understanding and make it complicit in the collaboration that is theatrical performance. They underscore the artifice of the stage by heightening the departure from verisimilitude. The more challenging and inventive the convention, the more privileged the audience's status. In *Translations*, the audience understands both English and Irish, which, with the exception of Owen/Rolland, the characters cannot. In *Philadelphia*, only the audience and Gar Public can see and hear Gar Private. Unlike his father or the other characters, the audience is in on the joke. The effect is its intimacy and identification with Gar.

On stage, direct address to the audience is often described by critics as inherently Brechtian – that is, as a dramatic technique for distancing or alienating the audience; direct address reminds audience members that it watches (and, in fact, participates in) the construction of an artificial reality on stage, not the mirror held up to nature, let alone the replication of real life. Theatre history abounds with precedents for such extra-dramatic narratives: the Greek chorus (of both tragedy and comedy), the Elizabethan soliloquy and aside, the music hall compère or Chairman (seen in Osborne's *The Entertainer* [1960], for instance) and the song. What is most distinctive about Michael's narration is that, like the voices in Eugene O'Neill's *Strange Interlude* (1928), it forces the audience to question how the individual's perceptions shape any discourse, any construction of the past, any version of the truth. Whereas the convention governing Shakespeare's use of soliloquy is predicated on the character telling the truth, or at least what that character perceives as the truth at that moment, Friel's use of direct address in *Dancing at Lughnasa* and elsewhere raises fundamental epistemological questions. How does a character (or, indeed, an audience member) know anything? Since memory entails an individual's reworking and unique understanding of experience, even before relating or communicating that experience through language, does the possibility of common understanding exist? This epistemological instability is central to Friel's dramaturgy and a key thematic concern. In *Philadelphia*, for instance, Gar Private challenges the discourse of other characters, especially by offering competing versions of the past. Gar Private sums up the central episode in that play in one of his cynical tirades:

> once upon a time a boy and his father sat in a blue boat on a lake on an afternoon in May, and on that afternoon a great beauty happened, a beauty that has haunted the boy ever since, because he wonders now did it really take place or did he imagine it.[94]

Gar's vividly recollected encounter with his father in the blue boat, which reappears in the *Lughnasa* film, strikes no chord with S. B. An alternative reading of *Faith Healer* suggests that, in accordance with conventions that govern the soliloquy, each character does tell what he or she believes to be the truth. The character's veracity is, thus, subordinate to, first, the way each constructs the past in memory and, second, the impossibility of objectively recreating the past.

On stage, Michael's narration, delivered in five addresses to the audience, comprises more than one-tenth of the play's lines. In addition to his introductory narration (BF, pp. 1–2), his recollection of Jack's return (BF, pp. 8–9) and the curtain speech before intermission (BF, pp. 41–42) appear in Act One. Towards the end of Act Two, the narration explains the departure of Rose and Agnes (BF, pp. 59–61) and concludes with Michael's final curtain speech (BF, pp. 70–71). Michael's narration – 'When I cast my mind back to the summer of 1936 different kinds of memories offer themselves to me'

– reveals that his memories exist not as a static, overarching narrative, but as competing episodes or fragments. Unlike the Commentators or Sir, Michael carries no written text, only contesting memories.

Michael's narration is attenuated and scattered throughout the film. In the screenplay and film, the more than 400 words in his opening narration are compressed to fewer than 50, interspersed throughout the first sequences. Removed by time and space from the grimmer aspects of the Mundys' fortunes, the stage narrator conveys a resigned acceptance of the past. The film audience knows only that 'they ended as shadows on the streets of London, scraping a living together, dying alone' (McG, p. 99), but not that 'they gave up. They took to drink; slept in parks, in doorways, on the Thames Embankment. Then Agnes died of exposure' (BF, p. 60). As played by Gerald McSorley in the original production, Michael's fatalistic resignation minimized sentimentality. Not only is the narrative stance lost in the film, so is the Brechtian alienation of having the adult Michael play himself as a child. Lost, too, are the framing but contrasting theatrical tableaux struck at the very beginning and end of the play. Posed carefully in Friel's stage directions, the characters are frozen in the formal tableaux as they are in Michael's different memories. As Prapassaree Kramer argues, the 'opening and closing tableaux particularly reveal Michael's judgments on his family and on himself, emphasizing his role as the creator and arranger of stage events, not just their record'.[95] Whereas the first suggests an idealized recollection of the past, the final tableau shows a shabbier reality.

Friel's dramatic monologues, Brechtian alienation techniques and doubled characters are essential to (and typical of) his dramaturgy. Not only do they challenge the dominant naturalistic conventions of twentieth-century drama but they are, by definition, incompatible with the invisible editing used to develop stable characters in a seamless, coherent narrative that is the hallmark of what Bordwell, Staiger and Thompson identify as Classical Hollywood Style.[96] The film's voice-over, a convention consonant with Classical Hollywood Style, readily accommodates and, in fact, co-opts the play's intimate yet alienating narration. Voice-over narration, especially when ironic in tone, is perhaps most familiar in *film noir*. The most celebrated examples include the narration by a dead man, seen floating in a pool in the opening sequence of Billy Wilder's *Sunset Boulevard* (1950), and by a series of putatively authoritative voices (newsreel narrator, unseen reporter) in Orson Welles's *Citizen Kane* (1941).

Cinematic voice-over narration, which grew out of inter-titles of silent film, evolved with the advent of sound. In documentaries, semi-documentaries and newsreels, the narrator assumed omniscience in 'the voice of God' narration. In fiction films, a character involved in the action provided voice-over narration in many of the classics of *film noir*, such as *The Maltese Falcon* (1941), *Double Indemnity* (1944), *Sunset Boulevard* and *D.O.A.* (1950), as well as more recent, non-*noir* films such as *Days of Heaven* (1978). Such narration established perspective, vested authority in the voice-over, bridged chronological gaps, supplied crucial exposition, made smooth transitions and created a trust (if not identification) between audience and narrator. The prevailing cinematic convention is that, if the voice-over addresses the audience, the character is not seen actually speaking the words of the narration. At the opening of *Sunset Boulevard* we hear Mike Gillis's voice, but we see his lifeless body floating face down in Norma Desmond's pool. Walter Neff's voice-over narration in *Double Indemnity* is dictated to Keyes' tape recorder (the action, in the person of Keyes, catches up with Neff's dictation at the very end of the film) and, in *D.O.A.*, the dying character tells his story in a hospital emergency room.

Instances of direct address to the camera/audience by a film character involved in the story are less common. In the best-known examples, *Alfie* (1966) and *Ferris Beuller's Day Off* (1986), the title characters (played by Michael Caine and Matthew Broderick) break the cinematic fourth wall to speak directly to the audience. Like the analogous theatre devices (soliloquy, monologue and narration), the cinematic direct address is reflective, even philosophical. By calling attention to its artificiality, direct address (as well as the use of out-takes in *Ferris*) also interrogates the nature of the medium. Ferris, for example, appears on screen after the 'final' credits have rolled to ask the audience why it is still in the theatre.

The adult Michael's voice-over in the film *Dancing at Lughnasa* conforms to the prevailing cinematic conventions of Classical Hollywood Style and raises neither the formalistic nor the epistemological issues of his stage counterpart. When the resigned voice of a young man on stage yielded to the sonorous voice-over narration in the film, reviewers found the latter overtly nostalgic, even maudlin. Stanley Kaufmann denounced Michael's narration as 'that most glib of devices, the voice-over' and the *Village Voice* disparaged it as 'so meretricious as to be offensive'.[97] Whereas Carlson describes the operation of memory in theatre as a process, on film voice-over narrative conveys an unaltering and unalterable certitude, in part because stage performance is subject to minute variations not possible on film.

5

DERELICT RITUAL

Irish drama and anthropology enjoyed a symbiotic relationship throughout the twentieth century. Synge's *The Aran Islands* (1907) and essays collected as 'In Wicklow,' 'West Kerry' and 'In the Congested Districts' have forceful anthropological motives and provided narrative inspiration for 'The Shadow of the Glen' (1903) and *The Playboy of the Western World* (1907).[98] The provenance of both narratives, specifically their authenticity as indigenously Irish, provoked enormous controversy. Eric Cross's study of a seanchaí and his wife in West Cork, *The Tailor and the Ansty* (1942; famously banned under the Censorship Act) was adapted for the stage by P. J. O'Connor and presented at the Abbey in 1968. Friel's interest in anthropology is evident in many of his sources as well as his edition of Charles McGlinchey's *The Last of that Name* (1986).

Cultural nationalists viewed anthropology as they viewed traditional music and dance, as defining an authentically Irish past. The Irish Folklore Commission, founded as a subsidized state agency in 1935, undertook the documentation of popular legends, traditions, beliefs and practices. In 1942, the commission surveyed hundreds of 'country-people' and from these questionnaires Máire MacNeill, daughter of Eoin MacNeill, compiled her definitive study, *The Festival of Lughnasa* (1962).

Like playwrights, anthropologists like MacNeill often focus on the rituals associated with pivotal times such as solstice and equinox, planting and harvest. In his study of ritual and theatre, Victor Turner noted the 'particular focus on calendrical and solstistial public ceremonies, such as first fruits, harvest, sowing, etc'.[99] Pre-Christian deities were associated with astronomical dates such as the solstices and equinoxes, as were Christian saints. In the Celtic calendar, quarterly days reflect the agrarian rhythm of the seasons: Imbolg (February 1); Beltaine (May 1); Lughnasa (August 1) and Samhain (November 1). (The second and last were taken as titles for the Irish Literary Theatre's publications at the beginning of the century and remain the best known.) Samhain was Christianized as All Saints' Eve and subsequently secularized as Hallowe'en. Midsummer's Eve and the Feast of St John the Baptist mark the summer solstice, which is still celebrated with bonfires that extend the light of longest day into the night. Some of the Celtic rituals surrounding Lughnasa were fully syncretized with Irish Catholicism. Like most cultural traditions, these Celtic festivals were fluid, since their survival was predicated on the ability to accommodate and fulfil the changing needs of their celebrants.

Lugh was the Irish variant of the Celtic god (Lugus) of light, sorcery, the crafts and the harvest. A warrior famed for his stealth, many skills and physical prowess, Lugh freed the Irish by turning Balor's evil eye on the dread Fomorians. The twelfth-century *The Book of the Dun Cow* describes Lugh as the 'divine father' of Cuchulain, who gestates the foetal child in his thigh and gives him the childhood name Setenta. The second book of Augusta Gregory's *Gods and Fighting Men* (1904), 'Lugh of the Long Hand', recounts the birth of Lugh, the exaction of the *wergeld* (blood money) from his father's murderers and his victory in the Battle of Moytirra. No longer the warrior champion, Lugh is configured in *Dancing at Lughnasa* as a benevolent domestic deity associated with bounty, pleasure, dance and music. In the film, Jack recalls Lugh as 'god of light, god of music' (McG, p. 84).

The Feast of Lughnasa is known by scores of local and regional names: Cromdubh's Day; Lughnasa Day; Lough Sunday; Blaeberry or Bilberry Sunday: Mam Ean Sunday; Domhnach Cranndubh; Latiaran Sunday; Garlic Sunday; and Pattern Sunday.[100] Because of the multiplicity of names associated with it and because it 'did not remain joined to the eve and first day in August' (MacNeill, p. 11), Lughnasa became increasingly localized and obscure. In the agrarian cycle, Lughnasa designated the time to begin the harvest of the new season's crops. In one account from Sligo, Lughnasa is known as 'the Sunday of the New Potatoes' (MacNeill, p. 112) – a direct link with Jack's description of the Ryangan Feast of the New Yam and the Feast of the Sweet Cassava. In Britain, the analogous celebration is Big Sunday[101] or Lammas Sunday; the etymology of 'Lammas' – 'new loaf' – links it explicitly with the harvest as well as the Christian Eucharist. MacNeill records that, even into the twentieth century, there was disgrace associated with beginning the harvest – eating, that is, that year's plantings – before Lughnasa. The feasting and hospitality of Lughnasa acknowledged survival as well as the land's bounty: crops had proved sufficient to sustain life for another year; nature's cycle continued as the new harvest became available.

MacNeill records hundreds of extremely diverse and localized customs and practices associated with Lughnasa, but the most were communal, festive assemblies at strategic sites – at wells, on heights and by lakes and rivers – characterized by feasting, music and dancing. (Indeed, 'nas' means fair or assembly.) Typical, too, was a procession to the site, which sometimes interpolated Catholic saints, especially native Irish ones, and evolved as pilgrimages. The Puck (possibly after the Irish 'poc' for goat) Fair, held annually on 10, 11 and 12 August in Killorglin, County Clare, the annual fair in Ballycastle, Northern Ireland, and communal picnics were all variant descendants of Lughnasa celebrations. MacNeill describes Ulster celebrations as distinct in a manner crucial to *Dancing at Lughnasa*:

> [In Ulster] the assemblies on heights . . . show no signs of having been taken over by Christianity. The country-people did not think of them as having any religious significance and accepted them as traditional occasions for festive outings. It is quite remarkable that so many of them survived down through the centuries without the Church's blessing. This omission, it might be expected, would have permitted

a particularly interesting survival of custom and legend. To an extent this is so – but, perhaps because too easily recognisable pagan traits would tend to be disguised or disappear and because the assemblies did not acquire, in compensation, the grand theme of Christianity's victory over Paganism, the legends are haphazard and fragmentary. (MacNeill, p. 140)

Of the nine festive assemblies in Donegal that MacNeill reports, most focus on youth, courtship and matchmaking. An old fisherman described the one celebration in Gainmere on the Rosguill peninsula in Donegal as explicitly excluding the old: 'No old person was allowed to go up the hill . . . Young men competed in dancing and the one adjudged the winner could then choose any girl he wished to be his bride. The decision often led to fighting . . . and the parish priest intervened to put an end to it' (MacNeill, p. 142). Most of the Donegal Lughnasa celebrations had died out by the first or second decade of the twentieth century, although the ones at Crookalough, Inishowen, 'flourished up to about 1930' (MacNeill, p. 147). Ironically, it would be the eldest sister, Kate, who would have been the most likely of the sisters to participate in such festive assemblies.

Both film and play foreground the pagan elements of Lughnasa, but in very different ways. Kate repeatedly uses the word 'pagan' to describe what she sees as criminal, reprehensible, immoral and, more generally, non-Catholic. Agnes, for instance, primping in front of the broken mirror with Maggie, quotes Kate's censorious question, 'Do you want to make a pagan of yourself?' (McG, p. 3), and jokingly refers to Maggie and Chris as 'a right pair of pagans, the two of you' (McG, p. 4). Kate later dismisses Rose's report of Lughnasa bonfires as 'pagan practices' (BF, p. 17). In *The Marriage of Nurse Harding*, the novel that Kate brings Chris, Annie M. P. Smithson, the most popular fiction writer of the decade, uses the word as Kate does: 'She was a devout Catholic, good girl in every way and although working in the midst of much that was evil, amongst girls who were frankly pagan in their outlook'.[102] For Friel, however, as for Euripides, the pagan accommodates the human need for ritual, which can destabilize and destroy those who would deny that need.

The central features of the Lughnasa rituals represented in *Dancing at Lughnasa* are the harvesting of bilberries, dancing and the bonfires. The harvesting of bilberries is one of the most widespread and enduring of the Lughnasa customs. In *Dublin Made Me*, C. S. Andrews (b. 1901, Dublin) recalls his family's annual excursions: 'On the second Sunday in August, Frochan Sunday, we used [to] go up to Glendhu to collect frochans.'[103] Jack fondly recalls Lughnasa as the time when he would pick bilberries with his mother, who would then make a jam used throughout the year, a welcome addition to a bland diet. In other instances cited by MacNeill, boys presented girls with bracelets woven from the bilberry plants. Bilberries are still harvested in *Dancing at Lughnasa*, but the festive and communal components of the celebrations have vanished. (Agnes, in fact, ends up collecting the berries alone.) What remains of the Lughnasa rituals is cut off from the harvest celebrations and denies the possibility of accommodating the Celtic in the Catholic, the pagan in the proper.

MacNeill reports only three instances of bonfires associated with Lughnasa, one each from Meath, Kilkenny and Limerick. Again, the festive, communal nature of these gatherings is unlike those seen in *Dancing at Lughnasa*. In Kilkenny, for instance, boys would pick the berries and deliver them to a chosen girl, who would then bake them in a cake that was eaten during bonfire festivities. In Limerick, the festivities leading up to the bonfire included a priest offering an open-air Mass. Ballybeg, however, no longer sanctions the bonfires. The unsettling rumour of bonfires and a serious injury to a boy named Sweeney are reported by Rose on stage and Michael in the film. In *Dancing at Lughnasa*, these festive rituals have been dislodged, dislocated and discredited. The Mundy sisters might now find themselves excluded from the celebrations on the basis of motherhood (for Chris), occupation (for Kate), or age. Perhaps there is so much talk of potential partners for them precisely because it is Lughnasa, and in previous years, the courtship possibilities would have loomed large.

Other rituals underscore what the surviving Lughnasa rituals have lost. Jack vividly recalls cognate Ryangan rituals: 'It's a very exciting exhibition – that's not the word, is it? Demonstration? – no – show? No, no; what's the word I'm looking for? Spectacle? That's not it. The word to describe a sacred and mysterious . . . ? You have a ritual killing. You offer up sacrifice. You have dancing and incantation' (BF, p. 39). Only later does Jack remember the English word, ceremony. Indeed, one of the alternate titles that Friel considered for the play was *Ceremonies for Lughnasa*. The sacrifice of the Mass is precisely such a ceremony, although it has long been divested of its atavistic elements – cannibalism in particular.

So profound and unsatisfied is the need for ritual that the characters in *Dancing at Lughnasa* seize opportunities to construct their own makeshift ceremonies. Michael's narration at the end of Act

Plate 14. Uncle Jack and Gerry before exchanging hats

One describes such a ritual, an unconventional marriage between Chris and Gerry, absent from the screenplay and film:

> And although my mother and he didn't go through a conventional form of marriage, once more they danced together, witnessed by the unseen sisters. And this time it was a dance without music; just there, in ritual circles round and round . . . I watched the ceremony from behind that bush. (BF, p. 42)

Jack imports a Ryangan ritual in which he and Gerry exchange hats.[104] This overtly performative re-enactment embodies the distinctive characteristics of ritual: special clothing (Jack's crumpled white chaplain's uniform), stylized movement (Jack 'carries himself in military style' [BF p. 68/McG, p. 94]), strict protocol and symbolic action. In his narration of the ritual, Jack again serves as anthropologist: 'I place my possession on the ground . . . Now take three steps away from it . . . turn round once . . . the exchange is now formally and irrevocably complete' (BF, pp. 68–69/McG, p. 95). The scene is like a postmodern bricolage of cultural images: wearing his now shabby, ill-fitting British army uniform, Jack exchanges the ceremonial tricorn of the last British colonial governor of Uganda for Gerry's jaunty boater while Michael stands by holding a rugby ball ('what Welshmen play' [McG, p. 94]). As in his earlier observation that the Feast of the Assumption has correlatives in other mythologies, Jack values ritual as investing human action with hieratic meaning. But this transplanted, alien ritual will not take root, will not be repeated. The absence of joyous native ritual is a symptom of a cultural pathology in *Dancing at Lughnasa*. Not only has ritual lost its communal inclusiveness, but (like the old Celtic celebration) its proximity to everyday life has been suppressed.

In *Philadelphia, Here I Come!* Gar Private rages against the failures of Catholicism, epitomized by Canon O'Byrne's inability to 'translate all this loneliness, this groping, the dreadful bloody buffoonery into Christian terms that will make life bearable for us all'.[105] In *Dancing at Lughnasa*, Irish Catholicism has suppressed the Dionysian, the means of release, and lost its capacity for joyous ritual. Instead, the Church, in the person of Father Carlin, as played by John Kavanagh in O'Connor's film, embodies the narrow, myopic view that sees Jack as a failure and an apostate and his propensity towards ritual as a threat. In *Faith Healer*, Frank recalls his Welsh and Scottish venues as sites 'all identical, all derelict. Maybe in a corner a withered sheaf of wheat from a harvest thanksgiving of years ago or a fragment of a Christmas decoration across a window – relicts of abandoned rituals. Because the people we moved among were beyond that kind of celebration.'[106] Such abandoned rituals are all that remain of Lughnasa. Gone are the inclusively communal, ecstatic elements of ritual: in their place are scrupulous piety and religious obligations.

Carlin's brand of Catholicism has also lost its power to shape the seasons. In Friel's stage play, for instance, the three weeks that pass between Act One and Act Two would include August 15, the Feast of the Assumption. What Kate describes as a Holy Day of Obligation, Jack describes in more abstract (and engaging) terms as the feast of 'the goddess rising'. Catholicism has failed Jack and Jack has failed it by 'going native'. Although Kate often speaks of the day when Jack will again celebrate Mass, he never does. Several projected communal celebrations – one to welcome Jack home, 'a great public welcome for you – flags, bands, speeches, everything!' (BF, p. 17), or the Mundy sisters attending the Harvest Ball – never materialize. In *Dancing at Lughnasa*, Catholicism has dispensed with its celebratory ritual – its very capacity for joy, for release, for escape, for carnival.

The failure of and unmet need for ritual appears in contemporary plays as diverse as Jean Genet's *The Balcony* (1956) and Peter Shaffer's *The Royal Hunt of the Sun* (1964) and *Equus* (1973). Moreover, throughout the twentieth century, theatre practitioners sought to reforge the linkage of theatre and ritual. In 1938 Antonin Artaud's

'The Theatre of Cruelty' mapped a radical agenda to reclaim the ritual power of theatre, albeit a quite different one from that of *Dancing at Lughnasa*. Friel's mentor, Tyrone Guthrie, described the origins of theatre in ritual: 'The theatre is the direct descendant of fertility rites, war dances and all the corporate, ritual expression by means of which our primitive ancestors, often wiser than we, sought to relate themselves to God, or the gods, the great abstract forces which cannot be apprehended by reason, but in whose existence reason compels us to have faith.'[107] The contrast between Catholic and Celtic permeates *Dancing at Lughnasa*: the former has become repressive while the latter remains expressive; one is passive (the Mass would not be celebrated in the vernacular for another three decades) and observatory while the other is active and participatory; one designates Holy Days of Obligation, the other celebrates feast days. In *Dancing at Lughnasa*, rural Irish Catholicism has lost its joyous register and settled for a dour solemnity.

6

RECEPTION

Many features of Friel's career might have precluded his popularity, especially outside Ireland: a decade-long commitment to Field Day, his recurrent use of a remote Donegal setting, a challenging, innovative dramaturgy. Yet he is perhaps the most commercially successful of twentieth-century Irish playwrights.[108] Produced on five continents and translated into dozens of languages, the play *Dancing at Lughnasa* is among Friel's most popular works. That its screen adaptation proved unpopular with film audiences owes much to the difference between theatre-going and film-going and to the highly theatrical nature of his stage play.

Friel's first international success came in 1964, the year he returned from Minneapolis. *Philadelphia* opened at the Gaiety Theatre under the direction of Hilton Edwards as part of the Dublin Theatre Festival on 28 September 1964. With some substitutions in cast, that production ran in Dublin, toured the United States throughout 1965 and 1966, toured Britain and ran in London at the Lyric Theatre in 1967.[109] Over the course of four years, it was performed hundreds of times to thousands of people. The staging, promotion and booking of *Philadelphia* mark a decisive move away from a standing theatrical company performing plays in repertory and towards an international, even corporate, model. Such an internationally marketed production necessarily involved compromise. In *Philadelphia*, for instance, it meant that outside Ireland the actors employed a generic Irish rather than a distinctly Donegal accent.[110] *Philadelphia* was an extremely influential production because it not only established an international reputation for Friel, but it also proved that an inventive, non-realistic dramaturgy was no barrier to box-office success. Only a few Irish plays – those of Brendan Behan in particular – had achieved comparable popularity in the twentieth century before Friel's *Philadelphia*. These plays reshaped what the world, especially outside Ireland, would understand as Irish drama.

In 1980 Friel and the actor Stephen Rea co-founded the Field Day Theatre Company, whose scope and success they could not have imagined. Within a few years, Field Day's enterprises included annual theatrical productions, many of them Friel premières, multiple-venue tours in Ireland and Northern Ireland and London transfers. As a co-founder and principal playwright, Friel devoted much of his energy, creative and otherwise, to Field Day in the 1980s. By the late 1980s, as Marilynn Richtarik notes, 'the most paradoxical tension in the whole Field Day endeavour – the pursuit of an essentially political goal by non-political means'[111] had surfaced. Moreover, Robert F. Garrett contends 'that continual connection to Field Day would restrict the kind of drama he [Friel] might write and that, conversely, a separation might engender a kind of artist liberation'.[112] With Noel Pearson at the Abbey, Friel decided that Field Day would not première *Dancing at Lughnasa*.

When *Dancing at Lughnasa* opened on 24 April 1990, it was Friel's first play to première at the Abbey in more than a decade. Patrick Mason's production was perhaps even more popular with audiences than with reviewers. On 15 October 1990, the Abbey production transferred to the Lyttleton Theatre (part of Britain's Royal National Theatre) and on 25 March 1991 it transferred again to the Phoenix Theatre in the West End. Few Friel plays had received critical acclaim and commercial success in London, but the London reviews were overwhelmingly favourable. Initial reviews, like later scholarly criticism, focus on the nature and positioning of the sisters' dance. *New York Times* critic Mel Gussow found the dance of the sisters nothing less than a *coup de théâtre*; in London, Michael Coveney wrote that in the dance 'the stage sings, then blazes'; the dance confirmed Benedict Nightingale's sense that 'at such times we are in the thrall of as masterly a dramatist as the theatre possesses'.[113]

Dancing at Lughnasa was the seventh Friel work produced on Broadway. Four of those productions, including the world premières of *Faith Healer*, starring James Mason and directed by Jose Quintero, and *The Loves of Cass McGuire*, starring Ruth Gordon and directed by Hilton Edwards, were commercial failures with only twenty or fewer performances. In addition to the success of *Philadelphia* in 1966, a 1968 production of *Lovers* ran for 148 performances. Even with a very positive reception in Dublin and London, the success of *Dancing at Lughnasa* on Broadway was by no means assured. (Its success did nothing for *Wonderful Tennessee*, which closed after only nine performances in 1993; neither *Molly Sweeney* nor *Give Me Your Answer, Do!* were staged on Broadway.) *Dancing at Lughnasa* was Friel's first Broadway play in twelve years, since *Faith Healer* in 1979, and his first hit on Broadway in twenty-two years. *Dancing at Lughnasa* ran on Broadway for one year and one day, with 421 performances between 24 October 1991 and 25 October 1992. Even though Vincent Gardinia referred to it as *Dancing at Lasagna* at the Tony awards ceremony, the production received eight nominations and won in three categories: Best Play (Friel), Best Direction (Mason) and Best Actress (Featured Role–Play: Bríd Brennan).[114]

The Broadway success of *Dancing at Lughnasa* triggered revivals of other Friel plays. In April 1994, a production of *Faith Healer* with the same cast (Donal McCann, Judy Geeson and Ron Cook) as the successful 1992 Abbey revival played at the Royal Court and toured America. *Philadelphia* was revived in the West End and on Broadway (with Joe Dowling directing) later that same year. *Translations* appeared on Broadway in 1995. Since 1993, *Dancing at Lughnasa* has been produced by hundreds of professional, university and amateur companies. In the 1993–94 theatre season it was the most widely produced play in American professional theatre. Anecdotal evidence suggests that the sisters' dance, especially as performed by amateur companies, is rarely the frenzied release that Friel describes but, almost as if in anticipation of the film, a plaintive, lyrical expression.

Between the première of *Dancing at Lughnasa* in 1990 and the film's release in late 1998, Ireland experienced remarkable change. Favourable economic climates prevailed in much of Europe and the world, but so intense, so unexpected, was Irish economic prosperity during this period that it generated its own label: 'Celtic Tiger'.[115] Economic, social and demographic realities were thought to be irremediable improved: by the mid-1990s Ireland enjoyed the fastest-growing economy and youngest population in the European Union; unemployment fell drastically as Ireland saw 'the highest rate of employment growth and the highest proportion of the population employed in the history of the state';[116] per capita income in Ireland exceeded that in Britain for the first time. Since the film's release, the Gross Domestic Product in Ireland has exceeded the EU 15 average. The economic exigencies that dominated Irish life, especially rural life, began to recede as the boom's sustained effects penetrated the social strata. The most immediate benefits of the 'tiger economy' fell to the upper and middle classes, which in turn expanded discussion of the inequalities in Irish society, especially 'the difficulties of a fragmented state structure in handling the tensions arising from uneven internationalization of a society and growing inequality'.[117]

Perhaps most importantly, the migration pattern was reversed, with not only returning emigrants but refugees taking up residence in Ireland. In 1998, forced emigration and the permanent dispersal of the family no longer threatened film audiences as they had in the 1930s and even in the 1980s. Between the time of Friel's composition of *Dancing at Lughnasa* and its release as a film, migration underwent a watershed reversal of a centuries-old trend: whereas a net 43,900 people emigrated from Ireland in 1989, in 1998 there was a net immigration of 21,200.[118] One sure sign of this shift is found in two books by Fintan O'Toole published in the 1990s. In 1994, O'Toole's *Black Hole, Green Card: The Disappearance of Ireland* described centuries of emigration as creating profound instabilities in Ireland.

Three years later, in *The Ex-Isle of Erin*, O'Toole's emphasis fell less on the negative impact of the multi-national corporations in Ireland and more on the disproportionate role that the Irish played in global culture.

In the 1990s an anti-essentialist, inclusive conception of Ireland embraced its diasporic millions and eclipsed old pieties. On both sides of the Atlantic and even in Britain, things Irish were variously described as 'hip', 'in' and 'sexy'. In the cultural arena, the 1990s witnessed remarkable successes for Irish visual artists (Kathy Prendergast at the 1994 Venice Biennale, for instance) and popular music, but the most conspicuous successes may have been in the performing arts. On stage there were international successes for not only Friel but also McGuinness (*Someone Who'll Watch Over Me*), Marie Jones (*A Night in November*, 1994), Sebastian Barry (*The Steward of Christendom*, 1995) and Conor McPherson (*The Weir*, 1997). The New York Drama Critics' award for best foreign play went to Irish works four times in an eight-year stretch: *Aristocrats* in 1989, *Dancing at Lughnasa* in 1992, *Molly Sweeney* in 1996 and *Someone Who'll Watch Over Me* in 1993. In 1996, London's *Evening Standard* named Martin McDonagh the most promising playwright, an honour that went to Conor McPherson the next year. When the Abbey revived *Dancing at Lughnasa* in 1999, *Variety* identified it as 'the first transcendent cultural product of the 1990s'.[119] The hipness of all things Irish was nowhere more evident than in two wildly successful commercial ventures: *Angela's Ashes* and *Riverdance*.

Frank McCourt's *Angela's Ashes* (1996) became the most commercially popular memoir of Ireland, spending years on the bestseller lists in the US, Ireland, the UK and elsewhere. Born only months after Friel, McCourt drew heavily, and controversially, on his childhood. McCourt's memoir shares with *Dancing at Lughnasa* the perspective of a boy in a Depression-era setting in which the often-capricious authority of a puritanical religion and harsh economic realities have produced households in which men fail, are unable or refuse to contribute as providers. The tone of *Angela's Ashes* is struck in its now famous second paragraph:

> When I look back on my childhood I wonder how I survived at all. It was, of course, a miserable childhood: the happy childhood is hardly worth your while. Worse that the ordinary miserable childhood is the miserable Irish childhood, and worse yet is the miserable Irish Catholic childhood.[120]

Friel's tone could hardly be more different. Although the Mundys live in a home with neither running water nor electricity, they are a functional family living in relative happiness and stability. Whereas Friel infuses his framing narration with the candid acknowledgement of subjectivity and instability, McCourt's memoir was attacked for its inaccuracies.[121] The contrast between the two works can even be stated meteorologically: it rains incessantly, torrentially, in McCourt's Limerick, but, in Michael's memory, the sun shines on Mediterranean Donegal.

McCourt's memoir epitomizes the counter-narrative to emigration, traced by Aidan Arrowsmith through the works of Seán O'Faoláin, Edna O'Brien and Samuel Beckett.[122] *Angela's Ashes* celebrates McCourt's survival; his success comes in escaping Ireland. McCourt emphasizes privation and humiliation, Friel the family bonds. Despite their squabbles, frustrations and repression, the sisters are neither miserable nor desperate. When, for instance, Maggie has eight people to feed and only three eggs, rather than a scene of desperation the meal becomes a leisurely picnic featuring Eggs Ballybeg on toasted caraway bread. Whereas Friel might be accused of suppressing the hardships of Irish life in the 1930s, McCourt was seen to hyperbolize them.

The publishing phenomenon of *Angela's Ashes* paralleled the blockbuster success of *Riverdance*. What began as a brief intermission performance from the host country at the Eurovision Song Contest was to become a booking phenomenon. *Dancing at Lughnasa* is directly acknowledged as an inspiration in the programmes for both the London and New York productions:

> There is something about dance that transcends all national, linguistic and cultural boundaries. Those who saw Brian Friel's play, *Dancing at Lughnasa*, will vividly recall the moment when the women in that repressed rural setting of Donegal in the Thirties, suddenly began to dance.[123]

Indeed, the programme, promotional materials and publicity for *Riverdance*, as well as the show itself, all advanced the notion that dance was a means of escape and release throughout Irish history that spoke to all emigrants in a trans-global language. Fintan O'Toole wrote that 'There is something of this mixture of gaiety and desperation, of this dancing on the edge of destruction, about *Riverdance*, the phenomenally successful Irish dance show in which the razzle-dazzle and the spectacle, the sexiness and the celebration, are inextricable from a narrative of emigration, displacement and loss.' In both *Riverdance* and *Dancing at Lughnasa*, O'Toole found 'an element of hysteria and self-caricature, the shadow of both Catholic puritanism at home and of Stage Irish display abroad'.[124]

When *Riverdance – The Show* was first presented at the Point Theatre in Dublin, it was devoid of narrative segues. Its scrim was a mackerel sky on to which a red sun, a moon, a Dolmen tomb, wild geese and a stylized, ornamental plate were projected. The specifically Irish elements of the visual presentation, its costumes and Celtic interknotted lighting effects, were subdued in comparison with what was to come. By the time *Riverdance* reached the Hammersmith Apollo in London and Radio City Music Hall in New York, its scenic design, narration and direction enlarged the production to suit the enormous stages and immense audiences. Its Irish content grew more prominent as *Riverdance* became not only a celebration 'rescu[ing] Irish dancing from the cultural commissars',[125] but an encapsulation of Ireland's history. Its reimagination of national history reached out and found diasporic audiences by drawing heavily on elements shared with (and possibly lifted from) *Dancing at Lughnasa*: the Celtic deities, the harvest, the emigration. *Riverdance – The Show* acquired a deeply intoned narration that introduced its numbers (or scenes), such as 'Reel Around the Sun', 'Women of Ireland', 'Slip into Spring – The Harvest' and 'American Wake', and chronicled the touchstones of Irish experience: famine, diaspora, rebellion. From its beginning, *Riverdance* incorporated cognate international dance forms from Spain (flamenco) and America (tap) and originally featured American soloists (Jean Butler and Michael Flatley). Eventually, the production was cloned so that six companies simultaneously toured the world. The bad seeds of *Riverdance*, Flatley's rococo *Lord of the Dance* and its sequels, divested Irish dance of its specifically Irish qualities and, in so doing, attained breathtaking commodification. While the Stage Irish were associated with drunkenness, sloth and verbal dexterity, the chorus lines of *Riverdance* bespoke rude health, stamina and stomping self-assertion. In comparison to the chorus line of dozens of professional dancers defiantly asserting a version of energetic Irishness, the film's image of five middle-aged women moving through their homespun dance paled.

The film's distributor, Sony, oblivious to the expectations engendered by *Riverdance*, hoped to build a base of critical enthusiasm from festival reviewers before releasing the film widely. Its release was staggered over several months, beginning with its première on 4 September 1998 at the Telluride (Colorado) Film Festival, prior to screenings at the Venice and Toronto Film Festivals, the Irish première on 23 September and the British première on 4 December. In the US it opened to exclusive engagements in major cities before reaching a maximum distribution in 95 theatres across North America. From the outset, the release strategy followed the model that American distributors use for films they envision as contenders for Academy Awards: limited exposure at prestigious festivals to attract positive

for your consideration

best actress
Meryl Streep

"*Meryl Streep has made
many a grand acting
gesture in her career.
'Dancing at Lughnasa'
ranks with the best!*"
–Janet Maslin, THE NEW YORK TIMES

Dancing at Lughnasa

SONY PICTURES CLASSICS

Plate 15. Meryl Streep

reviews from influential critics, late-year openings in major cities so as
to position the film as a contender for Academy Award nominations,
limited release in major cities and this followed by wider release.

Initially, the release strategy seemed to be working. The
Hollywood trade paper, *Variety*, was optimistic about the film's 'legs':
'Given the work's cultural pedigree, fine cast led by Meryl Streep and
even the current vogue for things Irish, Sony Classics should be able
to position this as a solid class offering in the US'.[126] In early
December, the National Board of Review of Motion Pictures placed
the film in the year's top ten list. In an enthusiastic publicity
campaign, Sony ran four half-page 'For Your Consideration'
advertisements in *Variety* in early 1999 that urged voting members of
the Academy of Motion Pictures to nominate Meryl Streep for best
actress, both Kathy Burke and Catherine McCormack for best
supporting actress and Michael Gambon for best supporting actor.[127]
So confident of the film's American success was Bord Fáilte that its

launch of a marketing drive to promote holidays in Donegal coincided with the New York première.

In Ireland, the film was respectfully and often favourably reviewed. Dublin provided extensive press coverage of the play's adaptation for the screen with articles on the casting, arrival and every movement of Meryl Streep, her Irish ancestors and her return for the Irish première and the screenings in Glenties in County Donegal. In the *Irish Times* review, Michael Dwyer found the acting superb, as did most reviews both in and outside Ireland. Dwyer's acceptance that Kate loses her job because of declining enrolment and praise of Bill Whelan's 'elegant score [that] explodes into life to drive the exhilarating sequence when the sisters dance together' suggest a lack of familiarity with the stage play. In *Magill*, Seamus Hosey was 'convinced that not only has the transition from stage to screen been successful but Pat O'Connor has recreated the humour, the pathos, the exuberance and the tragedy of the original play into a totally

Plate 16. *Kathy Burke*

moving and satisfying film'.[128] Writing in *Film West*, Muiris MacConghail judged that the film 're-established [O'Connor's] reputation filmically and *Dancing at Lughnasa* can rest with *Cal* (1982) and *A Month in the Country* (1987) as a troika of films which shows his particular talents in handling people and landscapes together'.[129] Other Irish reviews were less enthusiastic. In *Film Ireland*, for instance, Donald Clarke spoke of 'a hole in the centre of the film where the heart of the play was' and described the final dance sequence as where 'the picture really falls flat on its face'.[130]

In Britain, negative reviews well outnumbered the mixed notices and a single positive review (Barry Norman on BSkyB). *The Guardian*, which enthusiastically chronicled Irish film and theatre throughout the 1990s, found the film 'plodding'. Reviews from the *Financial Times, Independent, Observer, Sunday Telegraph, Daily Mirror* and *Daily Express* were all negative.[131] *Sight and Sound* applauded Friel's decision to stay out of the filmmaking process and blamed O'Connor for a 'middlebrow, bland film, lacking in emotional and intellectual bite'. Claire Monk was especially offended by the treatment of landscape: 'The generic Oirish visual lyricism O'Connor imposes muffles the impact and interest of the larger themes. The landscape is treated as one big photo-opportunity'.[132]

Maeve Binchy's ebullient and well-timed paean to the film appeared in both the *New York Times* and the *Irish Times* before its release in either country. Thrilled with O'Connor's adaptation of her novel *Circle of Friends*, Binchy was no less enthusiastic about *Lughnasa*: 'It is a joy to see a movie like *Dancing at Lughnasa* because it makes us Irish women realise what a long and triumphant journey we have taken'.[133] Following Binchy's lead, Janet Maslin in the *New York Times* was very positive: 'Whatever the material loses in claustrophobic tension and foreboding, it benefits immeasurably from the glorious, untamed vistas and the quaint ambiance of the little Irish village seen here'.[134] Other American reviewers were less enthusiastic: David Armstrong in the *San Francisco Examiner* described Gerry's motorbike rides as 'more travelog [*sic*] than drama'[135] and Roger Ebert lamented that 'The closer you get to these characters, the less you sympathize with their plight and the more you grow impatient with them'.[136] Michael's narration was the subject of often vitriolic criticism. Of the ambivalent treatment of memory in his narration, Stanley Kauffman remarked: 'Either Friel is trying to paint a golden glow on his dark story as it fades away or else he is trying to show us how memory, especially that of childhood, can shape the past the way we wish it had been'.[137] Both possibilities move only in the direction of nostalgia and sentimentality and away from the destabilizing effect of the play's narration. The repositioned sisters' dance was also a target of criticism, as in the populist *Entertainment Weekly*: 'When the sisters finally let down their hair and kick up their clogs, their celebration, which is meant to send us out feeling good, is so gratuitously exultant that it's as if the cast of a leaden production of *Three Sisters* had suddenly turned into a Michael Flatley kickline'.[138]

Film scholars have all but ignored not only *Dancing at Lughnasa* but also O'Connor's *Circle of Friends*. In *Contemporary Irish Cinema: From 'The Quiet Man' to 'Dancing at Lughnasa'*, O'Connor's most recent Irish films are mentioned only in the filmography and he is only briefly discussed for *Fools of Fortune*. Similarly, Martin McLoone devotes twelve sentences in *Irish Film: The Emergence of a Contemporary Cinema* to O'Connor's five Irish films and the majority of those concern *The Ballroom of Romance*. Lance Pettitt groups *Dancing at Lughnasa* with a dwindling number of heritage films made in the 1990s. Perhaps, after the public veneration of Friel, Irish reviewers tempered their criticism of the film. Whereas *The Ballroom of Romance* and *Cal* were seen as daring and innovative in their day and *Fools of Fortune* was an ambitious undertaking, O'Connor's more recent Irish films, *Circle of Friends* and *Dancing at Lughnasa*, have been consigned by film scholars to near oblivion. Ruth Barton, for instance, sees the triumph of Benny (Minnie Driver) in *Circle of Friends* as 'getting a boyfriend despite being fat' and describes O'Connor's direction of *Dancing at Lughnasa* as 'typically leaden'.[139]

Dancing at Lughnasa arrived in the US when the North American market was glutted with Irish and British films, including what was at the time the highest grossing UK import up to that time, *The Full Monty* (1997). As Pearson acknowledged on the eve of the film's release, 'The big problem lately, in the last two years, is there's far, far too much material available. There's so many Irish and English films stacking up with no distribution in America'.[140] Of the films on the New York-based National Board of Review's Top Ten List for 1998, five had strong Irish or British ties: *Gods and Monsters*, *Elizabeth*, *The Butcher Boy*, *Shakespeare in Love* and *Dancing at Lughnasa*. To its detriment, *Dancing at Lughnasa* was comparatively reviewed with yet another import, *The Rise and Fall of Little Voice*.

A fluke in late 1998 and early 1999 was the success of the last faux-Irish film of the century, *Waking Ned* (released as *Waking Ned Devine* in the US). Shot on the Isle of Man and written and directed by Kirk Jones, the award-winning producer of the Absolut Vodka television commercials in Britain in the early 1990s, *Waking Ned* concerns the high jinks of quaint Irish villagers in Tullymore (County Morewest), who attempt to cash the winning lottery ticket purchased by a neighbour who has died. After discovering Ned dead, the winning ticket (already endorsed with his signature) clutched in his hand, the central character dreams that he and Ned are adrift in a boat in a sunlit cove. Ned offers to share his chicken dinner, a gesture taken to symbolize his intention to share his jackpot with the villagers. The plot hinges on all fifty-two residents signing a pact to divide the winnings in secrecy. Everyone agrees, except for one recalcitrant woman, self-described as 'an old, disabled person with no money', who plans to turn them all in and collect a reward for reporting fraud. Reprising Margaret Hamilton's role in *The Wizard of Oz* (1939) astride a motorized cart rather than a broom, she is the classic informer. *Waking Ned* ends happily when the returning parish priest loses control of his car, crashes into the phone box in which she has called the lotto office and hurls her and it over a cliff, so that the lotto money can buy them all love and happiness. A dreadful film, *Waking Ned* draws freely on clichéd images of the Irish. Old, skinny (sometimes nude) men ride motorcycles in extended chase sequences, commitments are sealed with a shot of whiskey, knowledge is imparted through dreams. Coincidentally, *Waking Ned* shares some elements found in *Dancing at Lughnasa* (an illegitimate child, the consoling landscape, an encroaching technology), but its 'micksploitation' is, like that of Edward Burns's *The Brothers McMullen* (1998), a measure of commercial cachet of all things Irish at the century's close. Hugely successful in the US as well as in Britain, *Waking Ned* attracted the Irish-Americans who ignored the less rollicking adventures of the Mundy sisters. Released contemporaneously with O'Connor's film, *Waking Ned* outgrossed *Dancing at Lughnasa* 10 to 1 in the US.

CONCLUSION

Non-musical stage plays rarely profit from cinematic adaptation, not least because the transition to the screen often undermines the theatrical elements that bring the play to life on stage. The success of recent Shakespeare adaptations such as *Richard III* (1995, directed by Richard Loncraine) and *Titus* (1999, directed by Julie Taymor) lies in the exploration of filmic techniques to realize stage conventions like the soliloquy. The film adaptations of *Equus* (1977, directed by Sidney Lumet) and *The Importance of Being Earnest* (1952, directed by Anthony Asquith, and 2002, directed by Oliver Parker), on the other hand, suggest that reverence for the stage play may inhibit rather than promote effective cinematic adaptation. Whereas the narration of *Dancing at Lughnasa* destabilizes the grounding in naturalistic action on stage, the narration of the film has precisely the opposite effect: it intensifies the authoritative nostalgia of Michael as an adult. The film's voice-over narration and multiple reprises (dance, song, the kite) fix the past. Its seamless editing, heavily orchestrated soundtrack and *mise en scène* euphemize the subversive, transgressive elements of the play. Its treatment of the sisters' dance subordinates their momentary gratification of the long-denied need for expressive ritual to the beauty of the landscape and the glow of nostalgia.

The commercial failure and critical neglect of *Dancing at Lughnasa* are due, in part, to the fact that much of the novelty that an Irish film would have had outside Ireland was lost in the years between the play's première and its release as a film. Whereas only a handful of Irish films were widely distributed in the UK and the US in the 1980s, more than a dozen reached an international market in the 1990s: *The Field* (1990), *The Commitments* (1991), *The Crying Game* (1992), *Into the West* (1992), *In the Name of the Father* (1992), *The Snapper* (1993), *Circle of Friends* (1995), *The Run of the Country* (1995),

The Van (1996), *Some Mother's Son* (1996), *Michael Collins* (1996), *The Boxer* (1998), *The Butcher Boy* (1998), *The General* (1998) and *Dancing at Lughnasa*. Along with more marginally Irish films such as *Hear My Song* (1991), *Far and Away* (1992), *The Playboys* (1992), *The Secret of Roan Inish* (1993) and *Waking Ned* (1998), these effectively eliminated the novelty of a film made and set in Ireland.

Among these films, *Dancing at Lughnasa* is ostensibly conservative in content and especially in form, but in fact challenges preconceptions about Ireland in the 1930s: some women did work outside the home; non-marital children and non-traditional family formations predate the 1990s; the threat of globalization beset rural Ireland decades ago. As eager as audiences may have been for images of a lost idyllic Ireland, there are many ways in which *Dancing at Lughnasa* interrogates Ireland's past and fails to conform to the pattern of the Irish heritage film.[141] Michael's illegitimacy, Chris's rejection of Gerry's ambiguous offer that she and Michael 'come away' with him, Father Carlin's vindictive cruelty and the absence of support from neighbours or the community all frustrate those in search of a conservative heritage film. The nostalgic longings for the past endemic to heritage cinema are undercut by the reality of emigration that was, at least for Rose and Agnes, a rejection of (and perhaps a desperate attempt to escape from) their severely restricted opportunities in Ireland. *Dancing at Lughnasa* is, moreover, fraught with ambiguities about the effects of technology, globalization and the encroachment of 'the filthy modern tide'.

No better pleased were film audiences in search of a cutting-edge exploration of the pathologies of de Valera's Ireland. The characters in the film, like their stage counterparts, bridled under the stern authority of Church, state and community, but *Dancing at Lughnasa* offers conflicting rather than unambiguous memories of Ireland in the 1930s. The tensions between the Mundys and the world outside their cottage are matched by tensions within the family. Each of the sisters is individualized and none is demonized. Although their way of life is seen as repressive, stultifying and moribund, the sisters, on screen as on stage, remain vibrant, complex and, to varying degrees, rebellious.

CREDITS

Title:	Dancing at Lughnasa
Director:	Pat O'Connor
Release Year:	1998
Production Company:	Ferndale Films, Capitol Films, Channel 4 Films, Bórd Scannán na hÉireann, RTE
Country:	Great Britain, Ireland

Cast:

Meryl Streep	Kate Mundy
Michael Gambon	Father Jack Mundy
Catherine McCormack	Christina Mundy
Kathy Burke	Maggie Mundy
Sophie Thompson	Rose Mundy
Bríd Brennan	Agnes Mundy
Rhys Ifans	Gerry Evans
Darrell Johnston	Michael Mundy
Lorcan Cranitch	Danny Bradley
Peter Gowen	Austin Morgan
Dawn Bradfield	Sophia McLoughlin
Marie Mullen	Vera McLoughlin
John Kavanagh	Father Carlin
Kate O'Toole	Chemist
Gerard McSorley	Narrator

Credits:

Pat O'Connor	Director
Noel Pearson	Producer
Brian Friel	Play by
Frank McGuinness	Screenplay
Bill Whelan	Music
Kenneth MacMillian B.S.C.	Director of Photography
Gerrit V. Folsom	Line Producer
Mark Geraghty	Production Designer
Joan Bergin	Costume Designer
Mary Sleway	Casting Director
Des Martin	Production Manager
Cathy Pearson	Location Manager

Donal Geraghty	Financial Controller
Robert Quinn	First Assistant Director
Libbie Barr	Script Supervisor
Judy Friel	Script Consultant
Anneliese O'Callaghan	Production Co-ordinator
Michael Saxton	Post Production Supervisor
Gillian Cody	Post Production Co-ordinator
Des Whelen	Camera Operator
John Conroy	Focus Puller
David Grennan	Clapper Loader
Luke Quigley	Camera Grip
Alan Butler	2nd Unit Focus Puller
John Ward, Alaister Rae	2nd Camera Operators
Suzanne Nicell	Second Assistant Director
Hannah Quinn	Third Assistant Director
Jennifer Duffy	Assistant Casting
Kieran Horgan	Sound Mixer
Noel Quinn	Boom Operator
Terry Pritchard	Supervising Art Director
Conor Devlin	Art Director
Clodagh Conroy	Art Director
Julie Busher	Art Department Research
Steve Mitchell	Scenic Artist
Humphrey Dixon	Editor
Mary Casey	First Assistant Editor
Gaye Lynch	Second Assistant Editor
Declan McGrath	Third Assistant Editor
Alice Manning	Trainee Assistant Editor
Jonathan Bates	Supervising Sound Editor
Alastair Sirkett	Assistant Sound Editor
Nick Lowe	Dialogue Editor
Annie Gould	Assistant Dialogue Editor
Michael Crouch	Foley Editor
Len Tremble	Assistant Foley Editor
Alan Duffy	Assistant Sound Editor
Eammon O'Higgins	Property Master
Sunny Mulligan	Prop Buyer
Running Time:	96 mins
Colour Code:	Colour
Colour system:	Technicolor

Notes

1. Mervyn Wall, 'Some Thoughts on the Abbey Theatre', *Ireland To-Day* (September 1936), p. 60.
2. Noel Pearson, quoted in Marion McKeone, *World of Hibernia*, Vol. 4, No. 3 (Winter 1998), p. 72.
3. David Bordwell, Janet Staiger and Kristin Thompson, *The Classical Hollywood Cinema: Film Style and Mode of Production to 1960* (New York: Columbia University Press, 1985).
4. According to *www.imdb.com*, the film earned $512,970 in the UK (by 18 October 1998) and $2.285 million in the US (by 11 April 1999) in theatrical release.
5. Brian Friel, quoted John Lahr, 'In *Dancing at Lughnasa*, Due on Broadway this Month, Brian Friel Celebrates Life's Pagan Joys', in *Brian Friel in Conversation*, ed. Paul Delaney (Ann Arbor: University of Michigan Press, 2000), p. 214.
6. Vivian Sobchack, 'What Is Film History?' *Spectator*, Vol. 20, No. 1 (Fall 1999/Winter 2000), pp. 19–20.
7. Brian Friel, quoted in Lahr, 'In *Dancing at Lughnasa*', p. 214.
8. Tom Kilroy, 'Friendship', *Irish University Review*, Vol. 29, No. 1 (Spring/Summer 1999), p. 88.
9. Box 51/647, Brian Friel Papers, NLI.
10. Brian Friel, quoted in Anon., 'Press Diary: Unsinkable Brian Friel', *Brian Friel in Conversation*, ed. Delaney, p. 78.
11. Brian Friel, 'Self-Portrait', in *Brian Friel: Essays, Diaries, Interviews: 1964–1999*, ed. Christopher Murray (London and New York: Faber and Faber, 1999), p. 38.
12. Brian Friel, 'Self-Portrait', in *Friel in Conversation*, ed. Delaney, p. 38.
13. Brian Friel, 'In Interview with Graham Morrison', in *Essays, Diaries, Interviews*, ed. Murray, p. 7.
14. Brian Friel, 'In Interview with Laurence Finnegan', in *Essays, Diaries, Interviews*, ed. Murray, p. 129.
15. Kevin Barry, John Andrews and Brian Friel, '*Translations* and *A Paper Landscape*', *The Crane Bag*, No. 7 (1983), pp. 118–124.
16. Brian Friel, '*Translations* and *A Paper Landscape*', p. 123. Also quoted in 'A Reply to J. H. Andrews', in *Essays, Diaries, Interviews*, ed. Murray, p. 118.
17. James Delingpole, 'How *Dancing at Lughnasa* Writer Put Glenties Squarely on the Map,' in *Friel in Conversation*, ed. Delaney, pp. 229–230.
18. Brian Friel, *Making History* (London and Boston: Faber and Faber, 1989), pp. 2, 8, 29 and 35.

19. Field Day Theatre Company, 'Preface', in *Ireland's Field Day* (Notre Dame, Indiana: University of Notre Dame Press, 1986), p. viii. A similar agenda characterizes the Irish Literary Revival. Likewise, Brian P. Kennedy in 'The Failure of the Cultural Republic: Ireland 1922–39', *Studies*, Vol. 88 (1992), describes the implementation of a comparable (but revised) agenda in the first decades after Independence: 'The Irish language, early Irish history and literature, folklore and songs were to be rehabilitated and restored to their rightful place at the core of Irish life' (p. 14).

20. Stewart Parker, 'Introduction', in *Three Plays for Ireland* (Birmingham: Oberon, 1989), pp. 13 and 9.

21. Benedetto Croce, *History as the Story of Liberty*, trans. Sylvia Sprigge (London: George Allen and Unwin, 1941), p. 19.

22. Brian Friel, 'In Interview with Paddy Agnew', in *Essays, Diaries, Interviews*, ed. Murray, p. 87.

23. Brian Friel, 'Extracts from a Sporadic Diary (1979): *Translations*', in *Essays, Diaries, Interviews*, ed. Murray, p. 75.

24. Brian Friel, 'Important Places: A Preface to Charles McGlinchey's *The Last of the Name*,' in *Essays, Diaries, Interviews*, ed. Murray, pp. 120–121. These sentences do not appear in the US edition of Friel's preface to McGlinchey's book.

25. Alvin Jackson, *Ireland: 1798–1998* (Oxford and Malden, MA: Blackwell, 1999), p. 295.

26. Fearghal McGarry, 'Ireland and the Spanish Civil War: a Regional Study', *Bullán*, Vol. 5, No. 1 (Summer/Fall 2000), p. 23.

27. See Richard Kearney, *Postnationalist Ireland: Politics, Culture, Philosophy* (London and New York: Routledge, 1997).

28. Terence Brown, *Ireland: a Social and Cultural History, 1922 to the Present*, 2nd ed. (Ithaca: Cornell University Press, 1985), p. 114.

29. Paul Scott Stanfield, *Yeats and Politics in the 1930s* (New York: St Martin's Press, 1988), p. 9.

30. Caitriona Clear, *Women of the House: Women's Household Work in Ireland 1926–1961* (Dublin: Irish Academic Press, 2000), p. 7.

31. Bronwen Walter, *Outsiders Inside: Whiteness, Place and Irish Women* (London and New York: Routledge, 2001), p. 16. A marriage bar was indeed introduced in 1932, at least partially in response to a worsening global economic depression. Similar marriage bars existed or were instituted in many American states in the 1930s and endured into the 1960s. Americans still capitalize the decade as the 'Great Depression'.

32. Brian Fallon, *An Age of Innocence: Irish Culture 1930–1960* (Dublin: Gill & Macmillan, 1998), p. 2.

33. Joost Augusteijn, 'Preface', in *Ireland in the 1930s: New Perspectives*, ed. Joost Augusteijn (Dublin: Four Courts, 1999), p. 7.

34. Clear, p. 132.

35. J. H. Whyte, *Church and State in Modern Ireland 1923–1970* (New York: Barnes and Noble, 1971), p. 56.

36. Maeve Binchy, 'Five Sisters Alone Against Their World', *New York Times*, Arts Section (13 September 1998), p. 64.

37. Brian Friel, *Dancing at Lughnasa* (London: Faber and Faber, 1990), p. 47, and Frank McGuinness, *Brian Friel's Dancing at Lughnasa* (London: Faber and Faber, 1998), p. 38. Parenthetical references given in the text refer to the play as 'BF' and the screenplay as 'McG'.

38. Seamus Deane, *Celtic Revivals* (London and Boston: Faber and Faber, 1985), p. 166.

39. Whyte, p. 31.

40. Conrad M. Arensberg and Solon T. Kimball, *Family and Community in Ireland*, 2nd ed. (Cambridge, MA: Harvard University Press, 1968), p. 210.

41. Arensberg and Kimball, p. 99.

42. Pauric Travers, '"There was Nothing for Me There": Irish Female Emigration, 1922–71', in *Irish Women and Irish Migration*, Vol. 4 of *The Irish World Wide: History, Heritage, Identity*, ed. Patrick O'Sullivan (London: Leicester University Press, 1995), p. 147.

43. J. J. Lee, *Ireland 1912–1985: Politics and Society* (Cambridge and New York: Cambridge University Press, 1989), p. 176.

44. James Dillon quoted in Lee, p. 377.

45. Lee, p. 377; Tom Inglis, *Moral Monopoly: The Rise and Fall of the Catholic Church in Modern Ireland*, 2nd ed. (Dublin: University College Dublin Press, 1998), p. 291.

46. Fintan O'Toole, *Black Hole, Green Card: The Disappearance of Ireland* (Dublin: New Island, 1994), p. 12.

47. Lee, p. 384.

48. Christopher Murray, *Twentieth-Century Irish Drama: Mirror Up to Nation* (Manchester and New York: Manchester University Press, 1997), p. 170.

49. Nicholas Grene, *The Politics of Irish Drama: Plays in Context from Boucicault to Friel* (Cambridge: Cambridge University Press, 1999), p. 239.

50. Robert Welch, *The Abbey Theatre 1899–1999: Form and Pressure* (Oxford: Oxford University Press, 1999), p. 225.

51. Brian Friel, *Faith Healer*, in *Selected Plays: Brian Friel*, ed. Seamus

Deane (Washington, DC: Catholic University of America Press, 1986), p. 366.

52. Binchy, p. 64.

53. In principle, Friel remains open to the possibility of film adaptation of his plays. Leah Schmidt (Friel's agent) to author, 19 July 2002.

54. Friel, quoted in Gussow, *Essays, Diaries, Interviews*, ed. Murray, p. 147.

55. 'Why is the playwright asked to entrust the realization of his plays in the hands of this interloper who has no demonstrable skills? . . . in their hearts the song they want heard is their song because this is their interpretation, this is their vision. It is a sorry pass.' 'Seven Notes for a Festival Programme' (1999), in *Essays, Diaries, Interviews*, ed. Murray, p. 177.

56. Friel, quoted in Lahr, 'In *Dancing at Lughnasa*', p. 216.

57. Brian Friel to Noel Pearson, 13 March 1991, Brian Friel Archive, NLI, CB 119.

58. *The Ballroom of Romance*, directed by Pat O'Connor. Trevor set his short story in the early 1970s, but accepted O'Connor's suggestion that the television film be set back in the 1950s.

59. Luke Gibbons, *Transformations in Irish Culture* (Cork: Cork University Press, 1996), p. 83.

60. Frank McGuinness, '*Faith Healer*: All the Dead Voices', *Irish University Review*, Vol. 29, No. 1 (Spring/Summer 1999), pp. 60–63.

61. As Hugh, the hedge-school master, tells the British officer Yolland: 'We feel closer to the warm Mediterranean. We tend to overlook your island.' Brian Friel, *Translations*, in *Selected Plays*, p. 417.

62. Pearson, quoted in 'Up Close and Personal', p. 72.

63. John Hill, 'Romanticism, Realism and Irish Cinema', in *Cinema and Ireland*, eds. Kevin Rockett, Luke Gibbons and John Hill (Syracuse: Syracuse University Press, 1988), p. 224.

64. Robert Ballagh quoted in Luke Gibbons, *Transformations in Irish Culture* (Cork: Cork University Press, 1996), p. 86.

65. Martin McLoone, *Irish Film: the Emergence of a Contemporary Cinema* (London: British Film Institute, 2000), p. 35.

66. Christine Hunt Mahony, 'Memory and Belonging: Irish Writers, Radio, and the Nation,' *New Hibernia Review/Iris Éireannach Nua*, Vol. 5, No. 1 (Spring 2001), p. 11.

67. Harry White, 'Brian Friel, Thomas Murphy and Use of Music in Contemporary Irish Drama', *Modern Drama*, Vol. 33, No. 4 (December 1990), p. 554.

68. Friel, *Philadelphia*, p. 89.

69. Friel, quoted in Lahr, 'In *Dancing at Lughnasa*', p. 215.

70. Martin McLoone, 'Music Hall Dope and British Propaganda? Cultural Identity and Early Broadcasting in Ireland', *Historical Journal of Film, Radio and Television*, Vol. 20, No. 3 (2000), p. 306.

71. Arensberg and Kimball, p. 196.

72. The other forms of dance most closely associated with rural Ireland are step dancing and set dancing, which are governed by elaborate rules: the latter necessarily involves a partner and the former, years of lessons and practice. In 'The Dance Halls', Flann O'Brien categorizes dances based on the price of admission: 'For any dance costing over five shillings, you must put on what is known as "immaculate evening dress". www.setdance.com/archive/the_dance_halls.html. A dance like the Harvest Ball falls in this category; both the cost and what the sisters would wear are discussed at length.

73. Box 51/641, Brian Friel Papers, NLI.

74. Archbishop Gilmartin quoted in Whyte, p. 25.

75. Helen Brennan, *The Story of Irish Dance* (Lanham, MD: Roberts Rinehart, 1999), p. 39.

76. Teresa Deevy, *Katie Roche*, in *Three Plays* (London: Macmillan, 1939), p. 11.

77. Whyte, p. 11.

78. 30 May 1989, Box 51/641, Brian Friel Papers, NLI.

79. Bríd Brennan, interview with author, 28 October 2002.

80. Friel, 'Seven Notes for a Festival Programme', in *Essays, Diaries, Interviews*, ed. Murray, p. 177.

81. Joseph Cunneen, 'Two Tales from Ireland', *National Catholic Reporter* (18 December 1998), p. 18.

82. A similar episode of dance occurs in Friel's next play, *Wonderful Tennessee*. Frank's 'Ballybeg epiphany', seen only by him, is remarkably similar: 'suddenly a dolphin rose up out of the sea. And for thirty seconds, maybe a minute, it danced for me. Like a faun, a satyr; with its manic, leering face. Danced with a deliberate, controlled, exquisite abandon. Leaping, twisting, tumbling, gyrating in wild and intricate contortions' (p. 59).

83. Mikhail Bakhtin, *Rabelais and His World*, trans. Hélène Iswolsky (Cambridge, MA and London: MIT Press, 1968), p. 10.

84. Friel, *Faith Healer*, p. 340.

85. E. R. Dodds, 'Introduction', in *Euripides: Bacchae*, 2nd ed. (Oxford: Clarendon, 1962), p. xiv.

86. Marvin Carlson, *The Haunted Stage: the Theatre as Memory Machine* (Ann Arbor: University of Michigan Press, 2001), p. 2.

87. Christopher Murray, '"Recording Tremors": Friel's *Dancing at Lughnasa* and the Uses of Tradition', in *Brian Friel: A Casebook*, ed. William Kerwin (New York: Garland, 1999), p. 30.

88. Tennessee Williams, *The Glass Menagerie*, in *Three Plays* (New York: New Directions, 1945), p. 5.

89. Williams, p. 4.

90. Friel, quoted in Gussow, in *Essays, Diaries, Interviews*, ed. Murray, p. 146.

91. Brian Friel, 'Winners', in *Lovers* (New York: Farrar, Straus and Giroux, 1968), p. 9.

92. Brian Friel, *Living Quarters* (London and Boston: Faber and Faber, 1978), p. 9.

93. Brian Friel, *The Loves of Cass McGuire* (New York: Farrar, Straus and Giroux, 1967), pp. 12–13.

94. Friel, *Philadelphia*, p. 89.

95. Prapassaree Kramer, '*Dancing at Lughnasa:* Unexcused Absence', *Modern Drama*, Vol. 43, No. 2 (Summer 2000), p. 172.

96. See Bordwell, Staiger and Thompson, *The Classical Hollywood Cinema*.

97. Stanley Kauffmann, 'Stanley Kauffmann on Films: Irish Interiors', *New Republic* (30 November 1998), p. 32; and Amy Taubin, 'The Jig Is Up', *Village Voice* (17 November 1998), p. 138.

98. In his chapter 'Synge's *Tristes Tropiques: The Aran Islands*', in *Irish Classics* (London: Granta, 2000), Declan Kiberd writes that 'All anthropologists seek to record the moment when the techniques of "our" society are brought to bear in a study of "theirs": but the interest that draws a person towards the study of a culture may in the end overwhelm many aspects of the self. That is what happens gradually through Synge's narrative' (p. 437).

99. In *The Anthropology of Performance* (New York: PAJ, 1998), Victor Turner seeks a common ground between the rituals of 'simpler' societies and the more deeply encoded use of theatre and allied forms of performance in technologically complex ones. He uses the term 'liminal' to refer to cultural performances whose 'whole *ritual process* constitutes a threshold between secular living and sacred living' (p. 26, his italics). Although the liminal is often described as a threshold or border, one that might be crossed when leaving an enclosed space for an open one, Turner draws directly on the term's etymology, which refers to separating the wheat from the chaff, the nourishing kernel from its protective layer. Cultural performances, he observes, are neither wholly affirmative nor purely celebratory: 'This

relationship [between mundane and the cultural performance] is not unidirectional and "positive" – in the sense that the performative genre merely "reflects" or "expresses" the social system or the cultural configuration . . . but that it is reciprocal and reflexive – in the sense that the performance is often a critique, direct or veiled, of the social life it grows out of, an evaluation (with lively possibilities of rejection) of the way society handles history' (pp. 21–22). Rituals are often a violent, abject expression of human nature that invert decorous, as well as aesthetic, standards.

100. Máire MacNeill, *The Festival of Lughnasa: A Study of the Survival of the Celtic Festival of the Beginning of Harvest* (London and New York: Oxford University Press, 1962), p. 52.

101. See Michael Dames, *The Silbury Treasure: The Great Goddess Rediscovered* (London: Thames and Hudson), 1976.

102. Annie M. P. Smithson, *The Marriage of Nurse Harding* (Dublin: Talbot, 1945), pp. 117–118. See also Elizabeth Russell, 'Themes in Popular Reading Material', in *Ireland in the 1930s: New Perspectives*, ed. Joost Augusteijn (Dublin: Four Courts, 1999), p. 27.

103. C. S. Andrews, *Dublin Made Me* (Dublin: Lilliput, 2001), p. 49.

104. Friel toyed with the idea of a distinctive headgear for several characters, but left only Jack and Gerry with hats. In the 1930s, argues Paul Scott Stanfield, 'de Valera's preference for the soft hat over the silk hat . . . acquired a political significance, and one could declare oneself by one's choice of headgear' (p. 16).

105. Friel, *Philadelphia*, p. 88.

106. Friel, *Faith Healer*, p. 332.

107. Tyrone Guthrie, *A Life in the Theatre* (London: Hamish Hamilton, 1961), p. 314.

108. Tom Kilroy recalls his first meeting with Friel as 'a master-class in how to negotiate the shark-infested waters that lap the front steps of theatres around Times Square' ('Friendship', p. 83).

109. *Philadelphia* received six Tony nominations in 1966: Friel for Best Play; both Donal Donnelly and Patrick Bedford for Best Actor (Dramatic); Éamon Kelly for Best Actor, Supporting or Featured (Dramatic); Mairin D. O'Sullivan for Best Actress, Supporting or Featured (Dramatic); and Hilton Edwards for Best Director (Dramatic). Although it won no awards, *Lovers* (1969) received three nominations: Friel for Best Play; Art Carney for Best Actor (Dramatic); and Anna Manahan for Best Actress, Supporting or Featured (Dramatic).

110. Éamon Kelly, *The Journeyman* (Boulder, CO: Marino, 1998), p. 84.

111. Marilynn Richtarik, *Acting Between the Lines: the Field Day Theatre Company and Irish Cultural Politics 1980–1984* (Oxford: Clarendon, 1994), pp. 244–245.

112. Robert F. Garrett, 'Beyond Field Day: Brian Friel's *Dancing at Lughnasa*', in *The State of Play: Irish Theatre in the 'Nineties*, ed. Eberhard Bort (Trier: Wissenschaftlicher Verlag, 1996), p. 82.

113. Gussow, in *Essays, Diaries, Interviews*, ed. Murray, p. 140; Coveney and Nightingale, '*Dancing at Lughnasa*', *London Theatre Record* (8–21 October 1990), pp. 1385 and 1393.

114. The remaining nominations were: Rosaleen Linehan and Dearbhla Molloy, both for Actress (Featured Role–Play); Joe Vanek for both Scenic Design and Costume Design; and Terry John Bates for Choreography.

115. Gibbons dates the term 'Celtic Tiger' to 1994 and attributes its coinage to the investment firm Morgan, Stanley. See Luke Gibbons, 'History, Therapy and the Celtic Tiger', in *Reinventing Ireland: Culture, Society and the Global Economy*, eds. Peadar Kirby, Luke Gibbons and Michael Cronin (London: Pluto, 2002), p. 105.

116. Seán Ó Riain, 'The Flexible Developmental State: Globalization, Information Technology, and the "Celtic Tiger"', *Politics and Society*, Vol. 28, No. 2 (June 2000), p. 157.

117. Ó Riain, p. 159.

118. http://migration.ucc.ie/irishmigrationinthe1990scharts.htm.

119. Anon, '"Dancing" Like It's 1990 in Eire', *Variety* (12 July 1999), p. 43.

120. Frank McCourt, *Angela's Ashes: a Memoir* (New York: Scribner, 1996), p. 11.

121. See, for instance, Roy Foster, 'Selling Irish Childhoods: Frank McCourt and Gerry Adams', in *The Irish Story: Telling Tales and Making It Up in Ireland* (London: Penguin, 2001), pp. 164–186; and Edward A. Hagan, 'Really an Alley Cat? *Angela's Ashes* and Critical Orthodoxy', *New Hibernia Review/Iris Éireannach Nua*, Vol. 4, No. 4 (Winter/Geimhreadh, 2000), pp. 39–52.

122. Aidan Arrowsmith, 'M/otherlands: Literature, Gender, Diasporic Identity', in *Ireland in Proximity: History, Gender, Space* (London and New York: Routledge, 1999), pp. 129–144.

123. Programme, *Riverdance*, Radio City Music Hall, New York (1997), p. 11.

124. O'Toole, *Ex-Isle*, p. 145.

125. Sam Smyth, *Riverdance* (London: Andre Deutsch, 1997), p. 15.

126. Todd McCarthy, review of *Dancing at Lughnasa*, *Variety* (14 September 1998), p. 38.

127. None was nominated. Bríd Brennan, the only Irish actor from the original Abbey production, won best actress in the Irish Film and Television Awards in November 1999.

128. Seamus Hosey, 'The Lughnasa Phenomenon', *Magill* (September 1998), p. 6.

129. Muiris MacConghail, '*Dancing at Lughnasa*', *Film West*, No. 34 (Winter 1997), p. 17.

130. Donald Clarke, 'Dancing at Lughnasa', *Film Ireland* (August/September 1998), pp. 32 and 33.

131. 'Crix' Picks', *Variety* (7–13 December 1998), p. 32.

132. Claire Monk, '*Dancing at Lughnasa*', *Sight and Sound* (December 1998), p. 42.

133. Binchy, p. 64.

134. Janet Maslin, '"Dancing at Lughnasa": Five Unmarried Sisters in Postcard Ireland', *New York Times* (13 November 1998), section E, p. 1.

135. David Armstrong, 'Solid Cast Gets It Right, but Opening up Friel's "Dancing" Was Misguided', Weekend Section *San Francisco Examiner* (25 December 1998), p. 5.

136. Roger Ebert, '*Dancing at Lughnasa*', *Chicago Sun-Times*, <www.suntimes.com/ebert/ebert_reviews/1998/12/122301.html>.

137. Stanley Kauffmann, 'Stanley Kauffmann on Films: Irish Interiors', *New Republic* (30 November 1998).

138. Owen Gleiberman, *Entertainment Weekly* (27 November 1998), p. 54.

139. Ruth Barton, 'Feisty Colleens and Faithful Sons: Gender in Irish Cinema', *Cineaste*, Vol. 24, Nos. 2/3 (1999) (Contemporary Irish Cinema Supplement), p. 44.

140. Noel Pearson, 'Home and Away', *Film Ireland* (August/September 1998), p. 18.

141. Ruth Barton describes Irish heritage films as embracing a 'nostalgically uncritical' view of the past, set in the 1950s or before in a rural locale that has eluded modernity. Such films reaffirm what Arensberg described as familism, and are presented in a realistic style appropriate to its conservative values.

Bibliography

Andrews, Elmer. *The Art of Brian Friel: Neither Reality Nor Dreams.* New York: St Martin's, 1995.

Andrews, C. S. *Dublin Made Me.* Dublin: Lilliput, 2001.

Arensberg, Conrad M. *The Irish Countryman: an Anthropological Study.* Gloucester, MA: Peter Smith, 1959.

——, and Solon T. Kimball. *Family and Community in Ireland.* 2nd edition. Cambridge, MA: Harvard University Press, 1968.

Arrowsmith, Aidan. 'M/otherlands: Literature, Gender, Diasporic Identity'; *Ireland in Proximity: History, Gender, Space,* Eds. Scott Brewster et al. London and New York: Routledge, 1999: 129–144.

Augusteijn, Joost. Ed. *Ireland in the 1930s: New Perspectives.* Dublin: Four Courts, 1999.

Bakhtin, Mikhail. *Rabelais and His World.* Trans. Hélène Iswolsky. Cambridge, MA, and London: MIT Press, 1968.

Barry, Frank. Ed. *Understanding Ireland's Economic Growth.* London: Macmillan, 1999.

Barry, Kevin, John Andrews and Brian Friel. '*Translations* and *A Paper Landscape.*' *The Crane Bag,* No. 7 (1983): 118–124.

Barton, Ruth. 'Feisty Colleens and Faithful Sons: Gender in Irish Cinema.' *Cineaste,* Vol. 24, Nos. 2/3 (1999) (Contemporary Irish Cinema Supplement): 40–45.

——. 'From History to Heritage: Some Recent Developments in Irish Cinema.' *Irish Review,* Vol. 21 (Autumn/Winter 1997): 41–56.

Binchy, Maeve. 'Five Sisters Alone Against Their World.' *New York Times,* 13 September 1998, Arts Section: 41 and 64.

Bordwell, David, Janet Staiger and Kristin Thompson. *The Classical Hollywood Cinema: Film Style and Mode of Production to 1960.* New York: Columbia University Press, 1985.

Brennan, Helen. *The Story of Irish Dance.* Lanham, MD: Roberts Rinehart, 1999.

Brown, Terence. *Ireland: a Social and Cultural History, 1922 to the Present.* Ithaca: Cornell University Press, 1985.

Carlson, Marvin. *The Haunted Stage: The Theatre as Memory Machine.* Ann Arbor: University of Michigan Press, 2001.

Clarke, Donald. 'Dancing at Lughnasa.' *Film Ireland* (August/September 1998): 32–33.

Clear, Caitriona. *Women of the House: Women's Household Work in Ireland 1926–1961.* Dublin: Irish Academic Press, 2000.

Corbett, Tony. *Brian Friel: Decoding the Language of the Tribe.* Dublin: Liffey, 2002.

Croce, Benedetto. *History as the Story of Liberty*, trans. Sylvia Sprigge. London: George Allen and Unwin, 1941.

Dames, Michael. *The Silbury Treasure: the Great Goddess Rediscovered*. London: Thames and Hudson, 1976.

Deane, Seamus. *Celtic Revivals*. London and Boston: Faber and Faber, 1985.

Deevy, Teresa. *Three Plays*. London: Macmillan, 1939.

Delaney, Paul. Ed. *Brian Friel in Conversation*. Ann Arbor: University of Michigan Press, 2000.

Dodds, E. R. *Euripides: Bacchae*. 2nd ed. Oxford: Clarendon, 1962.

Fallon, Brian. *An Age of Innocence: Irish Culture 1930–1960*. Dublin: Gill & Macmillan, 1998.

Field Day Theatre Company. *Ireland's Field Day*. Notre Dame, IN: University of Notre Dame Press, 1986.

Foster, Roy. *The Irish Story: Telling Tales and Making It Up in Ireland*. London and New York: Penguin, 2001.

Friel, Brian. *Dancing at Lughnasa*. London: Faber and Faber, 1990.

——. *The Enemy Within*. Dublin: Gallery, 1979.

——. *The Gentle Island*. London: Davis-Poynter, 1974.

——. *Give Me Your Answer, Do!* London and New York: Plume, 2000.

——. *Living Quarters*. London: Faber and Faber, 1978.

——. *Lovers*. New York: Farrar, Straus and Giroux, 1968.

——. *The Loves of Cass McGuire*. New York: Farrar, Straus and Giroux, 1967.

——. *Making History*. London and Boston: Faber and Faber, 1989.

——. *Molly Sweeney*. New York: Plume, 1995.

——. *Selected Plays: Brian Friel*. Ed. Seamus Deane. Washington, DC: Catholic University of America Press, 1986.

——. *Two Plays by Brian Friel: Crystal and Fox and The Mundy Scheme*. New York: Farrar, Straus and Giroux, 1970.

——. *Volunteers*. London: Faber and Faber, 1979.

——. *Wonderful Tennessee*. London: Faber and Faber, 1993.

Garrett, Robert F. 'Beyond Field Day: Brian Friel's *Dancing at Lughnasa*'. *The State of Play: Irish Theatre in the 'Nineties*, Ed. Eberhard Bort. Trier: Wissenschaftlicher Verlag, 1996: 75–87

Gibbons, Luke. *Transformations in Irish Culture*. Cork: Cork University Press, 1996.

——. 'History, Therapy and the Celtic Tiger'. *Reinventing Ireland: Culture, Society and the Global Economy*. Eds. Peadar Kirby, Luke Gibbons and Michael Cronin. London: Pluto, 2002: 89–106.

Gray, Michael. *Stills, Reels and Rushes: Ireland and the Irish in 20th Century Cinema*. Dublin: Blackhall, 1999.

Grene, Nicholas. *The Politics of Irish Drama: Plays in Context from Boucicault to Friel*. Cambridge: Cambridge University Press, 1999.

Guthrie, Tyrone. *In Various Directions: a View of Theatre*. New York: Macmillan, 1966.

———. *A Life in the Theatre*. London: Hamish Hamilton, 1961.

Hagan, Edward A. 'Really an Alley Cat? *Angela's Ashes* and Critical Orthodoxy.' *New Hibernia Review/Iris Éireannach Nua*, Vol. 4, No. 4 (Winter/Geimhreadh 2000): 39–52.

Hosey, Seamus. 'The Lughnasa Phenomenon.' *Magill* (September 1998): 6–8.

Inglis, Tom. *Moral Monopoly: The Rise and Fall of the Catholic Church in Modern Ireland*. 2nd Edition. Dublin: University College Dublin Press, 1998.

Jackson, Alvin. *Ireland: 1798–1998*. Oxford and Malden, MA: Blackwell, 1999.

Jauss, Hans Robert. *Towards an Aesthetic of Reception*. Trans. Timothy Bahti. Brighton: Harvester, 1982.

Kauffmann, Stanley. 'Stanley Kauffmann on Films: Irish Interiors.' *New Republic* (30 November 1998): 32.

Kearney, Richard. *Postnationalist Ireland: Politics, Culture, Philosophy*. London and New York: Routledge, 1997.

Kelly, Éamon. *The Journeyman*. Boulder, CO: Marino, 1998.

Kennedy, Brian P. 'The Failure of the Cultural Republic: Ireland 1922–39.' *Studies*, Vol. 88 (1992): 14–22.

Kerwin, William. Ed. *Brian Friel: A Casebook*. New York: Garland, 1999.

Kiberd, Declan. *Irish Classics*. London: Granta, 2000.

Kilroy, Tom. 'Friendship.' *Irish University Review*, Vol. 29, No. 1 (Spring/Summer 1999): 83–89.

Kramer, Prapassaree. '*Dancing at Lughnasa:* Unexcused Absence.' *Modern Drama*, Vol. 43, No. 2 (Summer 2000): 171–181.

Krause, David. 'The Failed Words of Brian Friel.' *Modern Drama*, Vol. 40, No. 3 (Fall 1997): 359–373.

Lee, J. J. *Ireland 1912–1985: Politics and Society*. Cambridge and New York: Cambridge University Press, 1989.

MacConghail, Muiris. '*Dancing at Lughnasa*.' *Film West*, No. 34 (Winter 1997): 16–17.

McCourt, Frank. *Angela's Ashes: a Memoir*. New York: Scribner, 1996.

McGarry, Fearghal. 'Ireland and the Spanish Civil War: a Regional Study.' *Bullán*, Vol. 5, No. 1 (Summer/Fall 2000): 23–47.

McGrath, F. C. 'Brian Friel and the Politics of the Anglo-Irish Language.' *Colby Quarterly*, Vol. 26, No. 4 (December 1990): 241–248.

——. *Brian Friel's (Post)Colonial Drama: Language, Illusion, and Politics.* Syracuse: Syracuse University Press, 1999.

——. 'Language, Myth, and History in the Later Plays of Brian Friel.' *Contemporary Literature*, Vol. 30, No. 4 (Winter 1989): 534–545.

McGuinness, Frank. *Brian Friel's Dancing at Lughnasa.* London: Faber and Faber, 1998.

——. *Factory Girls.* 2nd revised ed. Dublin: Wolfhound, 1988.

——. *Observe the Sons of Ulster Marching Towards the Somme.* London: Faber and Faber, 1986.

MacKillop, James. Ed. *Contemporary Irish Cinema: from 'The Quiet Man' to 'Dancing at Lughnasa'.* Syracuse: Syracuse University Press, 1999.

McLoone, Martin. *Irish Film: the Emergence of a Contemporary Cinema.* London: British Film Institute, 2000.

——. 'Music Hall Dope and British Propaganda? Cultural Identity and Early Broadcasting in Ireland.' *Historical Journal of Film, Radio and Television*, Vol. 20, No. 3 (2000): 301–315.

McMullan, Anna. '"In Touch with Some Otherness": Gender, Authority and the Body in *Dancing at Lughnasa*.' *Irish University Review*, Vol. 29, No. 1 (Spring/Summer 1999): 90–100.

MacNeill, Máire. *The Festival of Lughnasa: a Study of the Survival of the Celtic Festival of the Beginning of Harvest.* New York and Oxford: Oxford University Press, 1962.

Mahony, Christine Hunt. 'Memory and Belonging: Irish Writers, Radio, and the Nation.' *New Hibernia Review/Iris Éireannach Nua*, Vol. 5, No. 1 (Spring/Earrach 2001): 10–24.

Maslin, Janet. '"Dancing at Lughnasa": Five Unmarried Sisters in Postcard Ireland', *New York Times*, 13 November 1998: E1.

Maxwell, D. E. S. *Brian Friel.* Lewisburg, PA: Bucknell University Press, 1973.

Monk, Claire. 'Dancing at Lughnasa.' *Sight and Sound* (December 1998): 42.

Murray, Christopher. *Brian Friel: Essays, Diaries, Interviews: 1964–1999.* London: Faber and Faber, 1999.

——. *Twentieth-Century Irish Drama: Mirror Up to Nation.* Manchester and New York: Manchester University Press, 1997.

O'Brien, George. *Brian Friel: a Reference Guide 1962–1992.* New York: G. K. Hall, 1995.

Ó Cadháin, Máirtín. *The Road to Brightcity.* Trans. Eoghan O Tuairisc. Dublin: Poolbeg, 1981.

Ó Riain, Seán. 'The Flexible Developmental State: Globalization, Information Technology, and the "Celtic Tiger"'. *Politics and Society*, Vol. 28, No. 2 (June 2000): 157–193.

O'Toole, Fintan. *Black Hole, Green Card: The Disappearance of Ireland.* Dublin: New Island, 1994.

——. 'Unsuitable from a Distance: The Politics of *Riverdance*'. *The Ex-Isle of Erin.* Dublin: New Island, 1997.

Parker, Stewart. *Three Plays for Ireland.* Birmingham: Oberon, 1989.

Peacock, Alan J. Ed. *The Achievement of Brian Friel.* Ulster Editions and Monographs 4. Gerrards Cross: Colin Smythe, 1993.

Pearson, Noel. 'Home and Away.' *Film Ireland* (August/September 1998): 18–20.

Pettitt, Lance. *Screening Ireland: Film and Television Representation.* New York: St Martin's Press, 2000.

Pine, Richard. *The Diviner: The Art of Brian Friel.* Dublin: University College Dublin Press, 1999.

Richards, Shaun. 'In the Border Country: Greek Tragedy and Contemporary Irish Drama'. *Ritual Remembering: History, Myth and Politics in Anglo-Irish Drama*, eds. C. C. Barfoot and Rias van den Doel. Amsterdam: Rodopi, 1995.

——. 'Placed Identities for Placeless Times: Brian Friel and Post-Colonial Criticism.' *Irish University Review*, Vol. 27, No. 1 (Spring/Summer 1997): 55–68.

Richtarik, Marilynn J. *Acting Between the Lines: the Field Day Theatre Company and Irish Cultural Politics 1980–1984.* Oxford and New York: Clarendon, 1994.

Rockett, Kevin, Luke Gibbons and John Hill. *Cinema and Ireland.* Syracuse: Syracuse University Press, 1988.

Smithson, Annie M. P. *The Marriage of Nurse Harding.* Dublin: Talbot, 1945.

Smyth, Sam. *Riverdance.* London: Andre Deutsch, 1997.

Sobchack, Vivian. 'What Is Film History?' *Spectator*, Vol. 20, No. 1 (Fall 1999/Winter 2000): 8–22.

Stanfield, Paul Scott. *Yeats and Politics in the 1930s.* New York: St Martin's, 1988.

Taylor, Lawrence J. *Occasions of Faith: an Anthropology of Irish Catholics.* Philadelphia: University of Pennsylvania Press, 1995.

Tomkins, Joanne. 'Breaching the Body's Boundaries: Abjected Subject Position in Postcolonial Drama'. *Modern Drama*, Vol. 40, No. 4 (Winter 1997): 502–513.

Travers, Pauric. '"There was Nothing for Me There": Irish Female Emigration, 1922–71.' *Irish Women and Irish Migration.* Vol. 4 of *The Irish World Wide: History, Heritage, Identity.* Ed. Patrick O'Sullivan. London: Leicester University Press, 1995.

Turner, Victor. *The Anthropology of Performance.* New York: PAJ Publications, 1988.

——. *Dramas, Fields, and Metaphors: Symbolic Action in Human Society.* Ithaca, NY: Cornell University Press, 1974.

——. *From Ritual to Theatre: the Human Seriousness of Play.* New York: PAJ Publications, 1982.

Walter, Bronwen. *Outsiders Inside: Whiteness, Place and Irish Women.* London: Routledge, 2001.

Watt, Stephen, et al. Eds. *A Century of Irish Drama: Widening the Stage.* Bloomington: Indiana University Press, 2000.

Welch, Robert. *The Abbey Theatre 1899–1999: Form and Pressure.* Oxford: Oxford University Press, 1999.

White, Harry. 'Brian Friel, Thomas Murphy and Use of Music in Contemporary Irish Drama.' *Modern Drama*, Vol. 33, No. 4 (December 1990): 553–562.

Whyte, J. H. *Church and State in Modern Ireland 1923–1970.* New York: Barnes and Noble, 1971.

Williams, Tennessee. *Three Plays.* New York: New Directions, 1945.

Printed in the United Kingdom
by Lightning Source UK Ltd.
105545UKS00001B/1-129

9 781859 183618